Diary of a Superfluous Man

Diary of a

Superfluous Man

IVAN TURGENEV

Translation and Introduction by
DAVID PATTERSON

W · W · NORTON & COMPANY

NEW YORK · LONDON

First Edition

The text of this book is composed in Avanta, with display type set in Centaur.
Composition by the Haddon Craftsmen, Inc. Manufacturing by The Murray
Printing Company.

Library of Congress Cataloging in Publication Data

Turgenev, Ivan Sergeevich, 1818–1883.
  Diary of a superfluous man.

  Translation of: Dnevnik lishnego cheloveka.
  1. Turgenev, Ivan Sergeevich, 1818–1883   Translations,
English. I. Patterson, David.   II. Title.
PG3421.D58 1984 891.73′3 83-23691

ISBN 0-393-01862-8

W. W. Norton & Company, Inc.
500 Fifth Avenue, New York, N.Y. 10110
W. W. Norton & Company Ltd.
37 Great Russell Street, London WC1B 3NU

1 2 3 4 5 6 7 8 9 0

INTRODUCTION

*W*HEN IVAN TURGENEV (1818–83) published his *Diary of a Superfluous Man* in 1850 he created the paradigm for a character type that appears in his later fiction as well as in the works of other Russian authors. Elements of the superfluous man, however, also turn up in earlier works of literature. Traces of him may be recognized, for example, in Tentetnikov of Gogol's *Dead Souls* (1842), in Pechorin of Lermontov's *A Hero of Our Times* (1840), in Pushkin's *Eugene Onegin* (1831), and in Goethe's *Sorrows of Young Werther* (1774)—all of which had a profound influence on the young Turgenev. Figures reminiscent of the superfluous man may also be seen in Golyadkin of Dostoevsky's *Double* (1846) and in Bel'tov of Herzen's *Who Is Guilty?* (1847); further down the line of Russian literary history, this character type appears in Tolstoy's *Cossacks* (1863) in the figure of Olenin and is reflected in the title character of Chekhov's *Ivanov* (1887). More modern times have seen remnants of the superfluous man in Joseph K. of *The Trial* (1925) by Franz Kafka and in Meursault of *The Stranger* (1946) by Albert Camus, to cite just a couple of examples.

The superfluous man is a person whom society rejects as worthless and who in turn rejects society; he is a square peg shoved into a round hole, someone whom the world treats "like an unexpected and uninvited guest," as Chulkaturin expresses it in his diary. Once the superfluous man collides with his condition, he characteristically sinks into a state of inertia or beats his head against the wall of impotent anger; often, as in Chulkaturin's case, he develops a neurotic need to fail and finally a longing for death. Moving beyond the literary context, we may observe that the Russian nihilists, or *raznochintsy*, of the 1860s viewed the men of the forties as superfluous men. The nihilists themselves have also been placed in the category of superfluity, but with a difference: they felt compelled to engage in revolutionary activity, while the men of the forties, as depicted in literature, were capable only of a vague protest at best.

Turgenev worked on his *Diary of a Superfluous Man* at intervals throughout 1848 and 1849 during his stay in France; he completed it on 15 January 1850, and it was first published the following April in *Annals of the Fatherland*. This was not his initial treatment of a superfluous man, however; Chulkaturin of Turgenev's *Diary* closely resembles the main character in his "Hamlet of the Shchigrovsk Province," a satire on the Moscow intellectual circles of the forties. "Hamlet of the Shchigrovsk Province" is one of the tales included in Turgenev's *Sketches from a Sportsman's Notebook,* a work which also occupied him during this particular trip abroad (1847–50) and which largely consists of stories aimed directly or indirectly against serfdom. The *Sketches*, in fact, made a strong impression on the future Tsar Alexander II, who emancipated the serfs on 18 February 1861; Turgenev would later look upon this as his single most important achievement in life.

One of Turgenev's main reasons for going to France was to be near Pauline Viardot, a beautiful—and married—French singer and actress. Because of the demands of her touring schedule, however, he did not see her as often as he would have liked; subsequently, he spent a great deal of time visiting the Paris residence of Alexander Herzen, a Russian man of letters who was also concerned with the concept of the superfluous man, both from a literary and from a philosophical point of view. Turgenev's association with Herzen contributed, no doubt, to his interest in the superfluous man as a human problem, a problem which penetrates the depths of the human struggle to belong, to be at home in the world. He explored the problem not only in his *Diary of a Superfluous Man* but in later works as well, including *Rudin* (1856) and *First Love* (1860).

Turgenev once indicated that there is a great deal of himself in the unsuccessful lovers who appear in his fiction,* and failure in love is a significant feature of Turgenev's superfluous men. After all, what better symbol of a man's estrangement from the world than the fact that the avenues leading to love are closed to him? Turgenev's relationship with Pauline Viardot and her husband, Louis, may lie behind much of this. His relationship with the Viardots is itself reflected in his only full-length drama, *A Month in the Country,* a project which he undertook while living in Paris in 1849. Here the character Rakitin is Turgenev himself; Pauline's counterpart is Natalia Petrovna, the woman whom Rakitin loves and whose husband is Rakitin's close friend.

In the *Diary of a Superfluous Man* Chulkaturin may also contain a trace or two of the man who created him. Chulkaturin, for example, is an unsuccessful lover, and when the object of his love, Liza, fails in her love affair with Prince N——, she marries the one man who might otherwise have become Chulkaturin's friend. Like Chulkaturin, who is dying of consumption, Turgenev was often ill while in France, and in May of 1849 he contracted cholera. Moreover, when he was preparing for his return to Russia

*Leonard Schapiro, *Turgenev: His Life and Times* (New York: Random House, 1978), p. 75.

7

in the summer of 1850, he addressed a few farewell remarks to Pauline that are reminiscent of something Chulkaturin might have said to Liza: "We will remain friends, will we not?" And: "If you were willing to promise me in return that you will remember me—I believe I could more easily bear this absence—with a less heavy heart. . . ."* Finally, it will be noted that like his creator, Chulkaturin wrote about his frustrations.

For all the similarities between Turgenev and Chulkaturin, the differences between them are more profound and certainly more significant to an understanding of the fictional character. Chulkaturin's circle of acquaintances, for example, has grown so narrow that by the time he sets out to write his diary, the only ones around him are his doctor, his nurse Terent'evna, and his dog Trezor. Having lived out his few years in the narrow and lonely margins of life, he is left to face death virtually alone. To be sure, his mortality seems to be the one thing he has in common with the mainstream of the living, and in dying he finally lays hold of something that no longer marks him as a superfluous man. Yet in the light of the emotional death he suffered when Liza—his one contact with life—eluded him, his physical death is all but anticlimactic. It should be pointed out, nevertheless, that if he is superfluous, Chulkaturin is not petty; he holds no grudge against those among whom he could not find a place, as indicated by his dying words: "Live on, ye who live!"

*Quoted by Schapiro, p. 77.

Diary of a
Superfluous Man

The village of Ovech'i Vody
March 20, 18–

𝒯HE DOCTOR has just left me. I finally got it out of him! No matter how much he tried to evade the issue, he finally said what he was thinking. Yes, soon, very soon, I shall die. The ice on the rivers will break up, and, very likely with the last snow, I shall float away to . . . where? God knows! Off to the sea. Very well! If I am to die, then it is best to die in the spring. But isn't it ridiculous for me to begin my diary perhaps two weeks before my death? But what difference does that make? How is it that fourteen days are less than fourteen years or fourteen centuries? It is said that in the face of eternity everything amounts to nothing—indeed; but in that case eternity itself amounts to nothing. I seem to be slipping into speculation; that is a bad sign— could it be that I am afraid? It would be better for me to tell some story or other. I am forbidden to go out—it is damp and windy outside. What tale should I tell? A respectable man does not talk about his ailments; writing short stories or something of that sort is not in my line; I do not have the strength for discourses on exalted topics; I do not even have any interest in descriptions of the life around me. Yet to sit around and do nothing is so boring; to read is sheer idleness. Oh well, I'll just relate to myself the story of my life. Excellent idea! It is appropriate in the face of death and shouldn't be offensive to anyone. I begin.

I was born some thirty years ago to a family of rather wealthy landowners. My father was a compulsive gambler; my mother was a lady of character . . . a most virtuous lady. Only I have never known a woman who derived less satisfaction from her virtue. She buckled under the weight of her merits and tormented everyone, beginning with herself. Throughout the entire fifty years of her life she never once stopped to rest, never sat idly by; she was always busy, forever bustling about like an ant—and completely without purpose, which cannot be said of an ant. An implacable worm ate away at her day and night. Only once did I ever see her totally at peace, and that was when she lay in her coffin on the day after her death. As I looked down upon her, it seemed to me that on her face there was actually an expression of quiet astonishment; it was as if those half-parted lips, those sunken cheeks, those meek and motionless eyes were saying, "How good it is not to stir!" Yes, it must be good, so very good, to be free at last of the tormenting consciousness of life, free of the persistent and troubled sensations of existence! But that is beside the point.

My childhood was a bad and unhappy one. My mother and father both loved me, but that did not make things any easier for me. My father had no authority in his own house and no substance as a man, so irrevocably was he in the grip of that shameful and ruinous vice. He acknowledged his downfall, and since he did not have the strength to renounce his favorite passion, he at least tried to use his affectionate and simple demeanor, his deferring humility, to win the indulgence of his exemplary wife. My mother truly bore her unhappiness with the magnificence and splendor of that long-suffering virtue in which there is so much self-satisfied pride. She never reproached my father for anything; without saying a word she gave him the last of her money and paid his debts. He extolled her to her face and behind her back, but he did not like to stay home, and he offered me his caress only on the sly, as if he were afraid that he might contaminate me with his very presence. Yet at those times his distorted features took on an air of such kindness, the feverish smirk on his lips was replaced by such a tender smile, and the fine wrinkles around his hazel eyes beamed with such love that I automatically pressed my cheek to his cheek, damp and warm with tears. I would wipe away those tears with my handkerchief, and they would flow again, without effort, like water from a glass that was filled too full. I would start crying myself, and he would console me, patting me on the back with his hand and kissing me all over the face with his trembling lips. Even as I sit here now, some twenty years after his death, when I think of my poor father mute sobs rise in my throat and my heart throbs, throbs so heatedly and bitterly, ridden with such sad compassion, that it's as if it still had a long time to beat, as if there were something to feel compassion for!

My mother, on the other hand, always treated me in the same way, affectionately but coldly. Such mothers, just and moralizing, are frequently encountered in children's books. She loved me; but I did not love her. Yes! I shunned my virtuous mother and passionately loved my depraved father.

But that's enough for today. I have made a beginning, and there is no need for me to worry about the ending, whatever it may be. My illness will take care of that.

March 21

The weather is marvelous today. It is warm and fair; the sun is joyfully dancing over the melting snow; everything is glittering, steaming, dripping. The sparrows are crying out like crazy all around the dark, damp hedges; the humid air is sweetly yet terribly irritating to my chest. Spring, spring has come! I am sitting at the window looking out over a stream and onto a field. Oh, nature, nature! I love you so, but I came forth from your womb unfit even for life. Over there a cock sparrow is hopping about with his wings spread wide; he is crying out—and every sound of his voice, every ruffled feather on his little body, teems with strength and health. . . .

But what does all that mean? Nothing. He is healthy and has a right to sing out and ruffle his feathers, while I am sick and must die—and that's all there is to it. There is no point in saying anything more about it. Besides, tearful supplications to nature are so ridiculous one could die laughing. So let us return to the story.

As I said earlier, I had a very bad and unhappy childhood. I had no brothers or sisters. I was educated at home. Indeed, what would my dear mother have had to occupy her if I had been sent off to a boarding school or to a government institute? That is what children are for, to keep their parents from getting bored. For the most part we lived in the country; sometimes we went to Moscow. I had governors and tutors, as is the custom. A certain tearful, cadaverous German by the name of Riechmann remains especially memorable to me; fate had made him into an unusually melancholy and dejected creature, hopelessly consumed by an anguished longing for his distant homeland. In the terribly stifling air of the dark anteroom, which was utterly saturated with the sour odor of old kvass,* my unshaven caretaker Vasily, better known as the Goose, used to sit by the stove in his perennial coat of dark blue sackcloth; he would sit and play his trumps in a card game with Potap, the coachman, who was dressed in a renovated, foamy white sheepskin coat and indestructible, blackened boots. Mean-

*Kvass is a kind of beer, low in alcoholic content, made by fermenting mixed cereals.

14

while, on the other side of the partition, Riechmann would be singing:

> Herz, mein Herz, warum so traurig?
> Was bekümmert dich so sehr?
> 'S ist ja schön im fremden Land—
> Herz, mein Herz, was willst du mehr?*

After my father died we finally moved to Moscow. I was twelve years old at the time. My father died in the night of a stroke. I shall never forget that night. I was sleeping soundly, as nearly all children sleep; but I remember that even through my dreams I seemed to hear a heavy, labored breathing. Suddenly I felt someone grab me by the shoulders and shake me. I opened my eyes, and there was Vasily.

"What's the matter?"

"Come along, quickly. Aleksei Mikhailych is dying. . . ."

I bolt from my bed and into the bedroom like a madman. I look: my father is lying there with his head thrown back, all red in the face, painfully fighting for his breath. People with frightened faces crowd the doorways; in the anteroom someone asks in a hoarse voice, "Have they sent for the doctor?" Outside a horse is being led from the stable; the gate creaks; a tallow candle is burning on the floor. My mother is there too, overcome with grief, but careful not to lose her air of propriety or the consciousness of her own dignity.

I throw myself on my father's breast, hug him, and begin

* Heart, my heart, why so sad?
What is tormenting you so?
It's indeed wonderful in this foreign land—
Heart, my heart, what more do you desire?

stammering, "Papa, Papa . . ." He lies motionless and winces in a strange way. I look him in the face—unspeakable horror takes my breath away; I gasp with terror, like a bird seized by some rough hand. They drag me from the room and carry me away. Just the day before, as if he had a presentiment of his coming death, he had held me so passionately and with such sadness.

They sent for some disheveled, blear-eyed doctor who reeked of vodka. My father died under his knife, and on the very next day, utterly dumbfounded with grief, I stood with a candle in my hands before the table upon which his body lay, stupidly listening to the deep tones of the cantor's song, which was interrupted now and then by the feeble voice of the priest. Tears kept streaming down my cheeks, over my lips, onto my collar, and down the front of my shirt; consumed with tears, I stared intensely, without making a move, at my father's motionless face, as if expecting him to say something. Meanwhile my mother slowly bowed to the earth, slowly raised herself up again, and making the sign of the cross, she firmly pressed her fingers to her brow, to her shoulders, and to her body. Not a single thought passed through my mind; I grew heavy all over, and I felt that something terrible was taking place within me. . . . It was then that death looked me in the face and made its mark on me. . . .

After my father died we moved to Moscow for a very simple reason: our entire estate was sold at auction to pay off his debts —absolutely everything, with the exception of one little village, the very one in which I am now living out my splendid existence. I confess that even though I was quite young at the time, I grieved over the sale of our nest; well, actually I was saddened only by the sale of our garden park. Almost all my joyful memories are associated with that garden. There on one peaceful spring evening I buried my best friend, an old dog with a bobtail and crooked paws; its name was Trixie. There too I used to hide in the tall grass and eat stolen apples, red, sweet Novgorod apples. And there for the first time, through bushes filled with ripe raspberries, I saw the housemaid Klavdiya, who, despite her turned-up nose and her habit of laughing into her handkerchief, aroused in me such a tender passion that in her presence I could hardly breathe; my heart would come to a stop, and I could not utter a word. One day, on Easter Sunday, when it came her turn to kiss my lordly hand, I very nearly threw myself down to kiss her worn, goatskin shoes. My God! Has it really been twenty years since all this happened? Can it be that long since I rode my shaggy chestnut horse along our garden's old wattled hedge, rising up in the stirrups to pluck the two-colored leaves from the poplars? While a man is truly living, he has no sensation of his own life; like a sound, it becomes clear to him only a short time later.

Oh, my garden park; oh, those overgrown paths along the little pond! Oh, that sandy little spot beneath the decrepit dam where I used to catch minnows and carp! And you, oh towering birches, with your long, overhanging branches, those branches that hid the peasant on the country road as his sad song filtered through, interrupted now and then by the creaking jolts of his wooden cart —I send you my last farewell! . . . To you alone I stretch out my hands as I depart from life. I would love to inhale once more the bitter freshness of the wormwood, the sweet scent of the buckwheat cut in the fields of my birthplace; just once more I would love to hear in the distance the modest ringing of the cracked bell in our parish church; once more to lie in the shade of an oak tree on the slope of a familiar ravine; once more to follow with my eyes the movements of the wind as it rushes over the golden grass of our meadow in dark streaks. . . .

Ah, what's the use of all this? I cannot go on today anyway. Until tomorrow.

March 22

It is cold and cloudy again today. Such weather is much more appropriate. It goes well with my work. Yesterday many useless feelings and memories were aroused in me; they were completely out of place. It won't happen again. Emotional outbursts are like licorice root: when you take your first lick of it, it doesn't seem so bad, but then it leaves a bad taste in your mouth. I shall tell the story of my life simply and calmly.

And so we moved to Moscow. . . .

But something just occurred to me: is there really any point in telling the story of my life?

No, it is utterly pointless. . . . My life is no different from the lives of most other people. My parents' home, the university, employment in menial jobs, resignation from positions, a small circle of friends, rank poverty, modest pleasures, subservient occupations, modest desires—tell me, in heaven's name, who does not already know all about this? And the fact that I am writing for my own pleasure is all the more reason not to relate the story of my life; and if in my past there is nothing that strikes me as particularly happy or even as particularly sad, then there really cannot be anything in it that is noteworthy. It would be better for me to attempt to offer myself some account of my own character.

What sort of man am I? It will be pointed out to me that one does not ask such a thing. Agreed. But, you see, I am dying, for God's sake, I am dying; and in the face of death I really think I may be excused for wanting to find out what sort of bird I have been, so to speak.

I have devoted a great deal of thought to this important matter. And since, unlike people who are strongly convinced of their own merits, I feel no need to be bitter at my own expense, I must confess one thing: I have been an utterly superfluous man in the world or, if you will, an utterly superfluous bird. I shall explain what I mean by that tomorrow, because today I am coughing like an old sheep, and my nurse Terent'evna won't give me a moment's peace.

"Lie down, my dear," she tells me, "and have a sip of tea. . . ."

I know why she is bothering me: she wants some tea herself. All right, all right! Now that the end is near, why not let the poor old woman get everything she can out of her master? . . . While there is still time.

March 23

Winter has returned. Snow is coming down in large flakes.

Superfluous, superfluous . . . an excellent word I've come up with. The deeper I plunge into myself and the closer I examine the whole of my past life, the more I am convinced of the harsh truth of that expression. Superfluous—precisely so. The word does not apply to other people. . . . People are good and evil, intelligent and stupid, pleasant and unpleasant; but superfluous? No. Don't get me wrong; the universe could get along very well without these people too. . . . That is certain. But uselessness is not their primary trait, is not their distinguishing characteristic, and when you are speaking of them, the word "superfluous" is not the first thing that comes to mind. But . . . in my case only one word can be used to describe what I am: superfluous—pure and simple. A supernumerary man—that's all there is to it. It is quite clear that nature did not count on my making an appearance in this world; subsequently, she has treated me like an unexpected and uninvited guest. It wasn't for nothing that one joker, a great lover of card games, said of me that my mother must have passed me in the same way she might pass something else. Now I can talk about myself quite calmly, without any resentment. . . .

But all that is in the past. Throughout my entire life I have always found that my spot was taken, perhaps because I have always looked for my spot in the wrong places. Like all invalids, I have been skeptical, timid, and irritable. More than that, between my thoughts and my feelings—and the expression of those thoughts and feelings—there has always been some senseless, incomprehensible, and insurmountable obstacle; this has probably been the result of pointless egoism or of an unsuccessful arrangement of my personality. And whenever I made up my mind to overcome this obstacle by force, to break down this barrier, my movements, the expression on my face, my whole being, assumed a look of agonizing exertion: not only did I appear to be phony and artificial, but I actually became so. I sensed this myself and hastened to withdraw into myself. Precisely then a frightening turmoil would rise up within me. I examined and unraveled myself down to the last thread; I compared myself to others and recalled the slightest glances, the words people had spoken, people whom I wanted to impress. I viewed everything in the worst light and laughed spitefully at my pretension to "be like everyone else"— and suddenly, in the middle of my laughter, I would give up completely, fall into an absurd despair, and go back again to what

I was doing before. In a word, I was running around and getting nowhere, like a squirrel in a wheel. Entire days were spent in this agonizing and pointless endeavor. Tell me now, if you would, can such a man be of any possible use to anyone or anything? As for why such a thing has happened to me or what the reason behind this tedious preoccupation with myself may be, who knows? Who can say?

I remember one day when I was riding out from Moscow in a coach. The road was good, but the driver had hitched an extra horse to the usual team of four. This unhappy and utterly useless fifth member of the team always arouses a deep compassion within me, especially when I see how he is fastened to the front end with a short, thick rope that cuts unmercifully into his haunches, rubs against his tail, and forces him to run in a most unnatural manner, making his whole body take on the shape of a comma. I suggested to the driver that perhaps we could do just as well without the fifth horse. . . . He remained silent for a moment and then shook his head, giving the horse a dozen or so lashes across its thin back and distended belly—and, not without a grin, he remarked, "Well, you can see how he really just hangs on! What the hell is a man to do?"

I too have just been hanging on. . . . Fortunately, however, the way station is not far.

Superfluous . . . I promised to demonstrate the truth of my assertion, and I shall keep my promise. I do not think it is necessary to go into a thousand trivialities, daily occurrences, or other incidents which in the eyes of any thinking person would truly serve as irrefutable evidence in my favor—that is, in favor of my claim; it would be better for me to begin with a single event of conclusive significance, in the light of which no doubt will remain as to the accuracy of the word superfluous.

I repeat: I have no intention of going into details, but I cannot

21

silently pass over one rather curious and striking point, namely the strange way my friends treated me (yes, I too have had friends) every time I happened to run into them or even drop in to see them. They would become very uneasy; the way they would smile when they came up to me was not entirely natural; they would not look me in the eye or at my feet, as some people do, but would rather look mainly at my cheeks, quickly taking me by the hand and just as quickly blurting out, "Oh, hello, Chulkaturin!" (fate has assigned me such a surname).* Or they would say, "Oh, it's you, Chulkaturin," and then immediately step aside and just stand there for a while without moving, as if they were trying to remember something.

I have been able to take note of all this because I am not lacking in insight or powers of observation; generally I am not stupid; there are even times when some rather amusing and not altogether ordinary thoughts enter my head. But since I am a superfluous man who is locked up inside himself, I am terrified of expressing my thoughts, especially when I know beforehand that they will come out all wrong. Sometimes it even seems strange to me that people can speak so simply, so freely. . . . You may well wonder how such a thing is possible. I must admit, however, that there have been many times when I was itching to say something, in spite of my being locked up inside. But it was only in my youth that I actually pronounced the words; in my more mature years I have been able to restrain myself almost every time. Barely in a whisper I'll say to myself, "Come on now, keep your mouth shut for just a little while longer," and then I'll calm down. We are all experts at keeping quiet; our women are especially good at it. A noble Russian lady may sustain a silence so powerful that it can

* The name Chulkaturin is derived from *chulok*, which means "stocking."

make even a man who is prepared for such a spectacle break out in a cold sweat and tremble slightly all over. But that is beside the point, and it is not for me to criticize others. I shall move on to the story I promised to tell.

Several years ago, due to the coincidence of quite insignificant but for me very important circumstances, I happened to spend about six months in the town of O——, the main town in its district. The whole settlement is built on the side of a hill and is very poorly designed. It has around eight hundred inhabitants who are utterly destitute and who live in hovels unlike any others I have ever seen. Here and there, through the pretension of pavement they call main street, white slabs of uncut limestone protrude so much that the peasants have to drive their carts around them. In the center of an amazingly filthy square a small yellow structure with dark holes juts up from the ground, and people wearing caps with large visors sit in the holes and pretend to be engaged in some trade or other; there too an unusually long pole of many colors towers up into the air, and a pile of yellow hay is kept around the pole by order of the authorities, with a hen belonging to the State policing the area. In a word, the town of O—— is marvelous, simply marvelous.

On the first day of my stay in this town I very nearly went out of my mind from boredom. I must say of myself that even though I am indeed a superfluous man, it is not of my own volition; although I am sick myself, I cannot tolerate anyone or anything else that is sick. . . . I have nothing against happiness; in fact, I have tried to approach it from every angle. . . . So it should not be surprising that I can experience boredom like any other mortal. I was in the town of O—— on official government business. . . .

I swear, Terent'evna is absolutely determined to kill me. Here is an example of our conversation:

Terent'evna. Oh, my dear, why do you go on writing so much? It's bad for your health to write so.

I. But I'm bored, Terent'evna!

She. You need to have a sip of tea and lie down. God knows, you're working too hard; come on now and take a nap.

I. But I don't want to go to sleep.

She. Oh, my dear, why do you talk that way? Lord be with you, lie now, just for a bit. You'll feel better.

I. I'm going to die anyway, Terent'evna!

She. The Lord protect you and have mercy. . . . Well then, are you ordering me to make some tea?

I. Terent'evna, I shall not live out the week!

She. Ah, my dear, why do you talk that way? . . . I'll go get the samovar ready.

Oh, you sickly, broken-down, toothless creature! Is it possible that you too do not take me for a human being?

March 24. A hard frost.

On the very day of my arrival in the town of O——, the government business I mentioned above took me to the home of a man named Ozhogin, Kirilla Matveich Ozhogin, one of the district's highest officials. I got to know him quite well after only two weeks, or, as the saying goes, I came to be on intimate terms with him. His house was located on the main street; it was distinguished from the other houses by its size, its painted roof, and the two lions on either side of the gate, two members of that race of lions which bear a striking resemblance to dogs bred in Moscow that did not

turn out well. From these lions alone one could see that Ozhogin
was a wealthy man. To be sure, he owned the souls of four hundred
serfs; he entertained the very best of the town's society and was
known for his hospitality. The chief of police visited him, riding
in a broad, reddish carriage drawn by a pair of horses; he was an
unusually big, strong man who looked as if he had been carved out
of some ancient substance. Ozhogin also had visits from other
officials: the local lawyer, a pale, rather malicious creature; the
communications officer, a gentle soul, a singer, but given to gossip;
the former district chief, a gentleman who dyed his hair and who
wore wrinkled shirts, tight pants, and that noble facial expression
that characterizes people who have been to court. Then there were
the two landowners, inseparable friends, neither of whom was
young—in fact, each of them had one foot in the grave. The
younger of the two was constantly censuring the elder, forever
shutting him up with the same reproach: "That's enough, Sergei
Sergeich. What do you know about it? After all, you write the
word *probka** with a *b* instead of a *p*. Yes, gentlemen," he would
continue with heated conviction, turning to those present, "Sergei
Sergeich does not write *probka*, but *brobka*."

And everyone there would laugh, although it is doubtful that
any of them were particularly skilled at the art of handwriting; the
unhappy Sergei Sergeich would then fall silent and bow his head
with a timid smile. But I am slipping into too many details,
forgetting that my days are numbered. So without wasting any
more time: Ozhogin was married and had a daughter named
Elizaveta Kirillovna, and I fell in love with her.

Ozhogin himself was a common sort of man, neither good nor

Probka means "cork." It may also be noted that when describing a particularly
asinine person, the Russians will say, "He is as stupid as a cork"—*On glup, kak
probka*.

bad; his wife was beginning to look more and more like an old hen; but their daughter did not take after her parents. She was very good-natured, gentle and full of life. Her bright, gray eyes beamed with kindness and looked straight ahead from under brows that were arched in a childlike manner; she smiled almost constantly and was given to laughter. Her refreshing voice had a pleasant sound; she moved about freely, gracefully, and had a cheerful way of blushing. She did not dress too extravagantly; the most simple clothes suited her best.

Generally I have not made friends very quickly, yet if I feel at ease with someone the first time we meet—which, by the way, has almost never happened—I must admit that it has been very favorable to the relationship. I have never known how to behave around women at all, and in their presence I have either frowned and looked furious or shown them my teeth in the most stupid grin, twisting and turning my tongue about my mouth in confusion. With Elizaveta Kirillovna, however, I felt completely at ease from the very beginning. This is how it happened.

I arrive at Ozhogin's just before dinner one day and ask, "Is he home?"

"Yes, he is," the servant tells me. "He is getting dressed. Please come into the drawing room."

I go into the drawing room. I look. Next to the window, with her back turned to me, is a young girl in a white dress; she is holding a cage in her hands.

I shrink back a little, out of habit; I cough, nevertheless, for the sake of propriety. The girl quickly turns around, so quickly that the locks of her hair brush across her face. She sees me, bows, and with a smile shows me the little cage box; it is half full of seed.

"Will you allow me?"

Needless to say, I keep to what is proper under such circum-

stances from the start, bowing my head while at the same time
buckling and straightening my knees (as if someone has hit the
back of my legs from behind); as everyone knows, this serves as
an indication of excellent breeding, grace, and charm. Then I
smile, raise my hand, and cautiously but gently wave it in the air
a couple of times. The girl immediately turns away from me, takes
a small plank from the cage, and begins scraping it violently with
a knife; then suddenly, without changing her position, she pro-
nounces the following words: "This is Papa's bullfinch. . . . Do you
like bullfinches?"

"I prefer canaries," I reply, not without a certain amount of
effort.

"Ah, I like canaries too. But just look at him; isn't he pretty?
See, he isn't afraid." (What surprises me is the fact that I am not
afraid.) "Come closer. His name is Popka."

I draw closer and bend over to look.

"Isn't he darling?"

She turns her face toward me; but we are standing so close to
each other that she has to bend her head back a little just to look
at me with her delicate, shining eyes. I gaze at her; the whole of
her young, rosy face smiles in such a friendly way that I smile back
and can hardly keep from laughing with joy.

The door opens; Mr. Ozhogin walks in. I immediately go up
to him and start talking to him openly and easily. I do not know
myself how I happened to join them for dinner and then stay on
for the rest of the evening. And the next day Ozhogin's servant
—a lanky, nearsighted fellow—was already smiling at me as if I
were a friend of the family when he helped me off with my
overcoat.

To find a refuge, to build myself even a temporary nest, to
know the joy of daily relationships and routines—this was a happi-

ness that I, as a superfluous man with no family memories, had never experienced until that time. If there were anything about me suggestive of a flower, and if such a comparison were not so worn out, I might declare that from that day on my soul began to blossom. Everything within me and around me went through such a sudden transformation! My entire life was illuminated by love, all of it, down to the slightest detail; it was as though a candle had been brought into a dark, deserted room. I went to bed, got up in the morning, dressed, had breakfast, smoked my pipe—all in a way that was different from before; I even skipped as I walked —really I did, as if wings had suddenly sprouted from my shoulders. I remember that never for a moment did I have any doubts about the feeling Elizaveta Kirillovna had inspired within me: I fell passionately in love with her on the first day we met, and from that very first day I knew that I was in love. I saw her very day over the next three weeks. Those three weeks were the happiest time of my life; but the memory of them is painful to me. I am unable to think of them without thinking of something else: quite against my will I am reminded of what followed those three weeks, and malicious bitterness slowly grips the heart that has just grown soft.

Everyone knows that when a man is feeling well his brain is not very active. A feeling of peace and joy, a feeling of satisfaction, permeates his whole being; he is encompassed by it; his sense of individuality disappears—he is in a state of bliss, as poorly educated poets would say. But when the "spell" finally wears off, the man sometimes feels deeply disappointed and regrets that in the midst of his happiness he failed to take a closer look at himself, that he did not double his reflection and his memories, that he did not prolong his enjoyment . . . as if there could ever be a "blissful" man, or any point in reflecting on one's feelings! A happy man is like a fly in the sunshine. That is why it is nearly impossible for me to hold on to any clear or definite impressions when I think back on those three weeks; the fact that during all that time nothing especially noteworthy happened between us makes it all the more difficult for me. . . . I look upon those twenty days as something warm, young, and fragrant, a kind of bright spot in my dull, gray life. My memory becomes inexorably faithful and clear only from the moment when the blows of fate began to rain down upon me, to put it as those same badly educated writers might.

Yes, those three weeks . . . Actually, they have not left me without any impressions at all. Whenever I happen to think about those days for a long time, various memories rise up from the darkness of the past—like stars emerging unexpectedly from the evening sky to catch the eyes of those who eagerly seek them out. Especially memorable to me is a certain stroll through a grove outside of town. There were four of us: Mme Ozhogin, Liza, myself, and a certain Biz'menkov, one of the town's minor officials, a fair-haired, kind, and humble man. I shall have occasion to say more about him later. Mr. Ozhogin stayed home; he had a headache from sleeping too long. It was a wonderful day, warm and calm.

It should be pointed out that parks designed for amusement and taking walks in public are not to the Russian's taste. In the so-called public gardens of the governmental towns you will never meet a single living soul, no matter what time of year it may be; some old woman might sit down with a moan on a green park bench baked through and through by the sun next to a diseased tree, and even then it is only because there is no dirty little shop nearby. But if there is a sparse little birch grove in the vicinity of the town, the merchants and sometimes the local officials will gladly go there on Sundays and holidays with their samovars, pies, and watermelons; they'll arrange all this bounty on the dusty grass right next to the road, seat themselves all around it, and eat and drink tea in the sweat of their brows on into the evening.

There was just such a grove about two versts* outside the town of O———. We went there after dinner, had our proper cup of tea, and then all four of us set out to take a walk in the grove. Biz'menkov offered his arm to Mme Ozhogin; I gave mine to Liza. The afternoon was already approaching evening. At the time I was wrapped up in the heat of first love (no more than two weeks had passed since we first met). It was a state of passionate and intense adoration in which your whole soul innocently and involuntarily follows every movement of the one you love; in which you cannot get enough of her presence or hear enough of her voice; in which you smile and look like a convalescent child, and a man with any experience at all can tell at a glance, even from a hundred paces, exactly what is happening to you.

Until that day I had never once had the chance to take Liza's arm. We went along side by side, quietly walking through the green grass. A light breeze was fluttering around us and between the trunks of the birch trees; now and then a ribbon from her hat blew across my face. I stared at her intensely, until at last she gave me a cheerful glance, and we smiled at each other. The birds overhead chirped their approval; the light blue sky peeked tenderly through the delicate leaves. My head reeled from too much pleasure. One thing must quickly be noted: Liza was not the least bit in love with me. She liked me; generally she was not shy around anybody, but I was not to be the one chosen to disturb her childlike tranquillity. She walked arm in arm with me as she would with a brother. She was seventeen years old at the time. . . . And

*One verst is just over two-thirds of a mile.

yet that very evening, right before my eyes, that silent
fermentation began to take place within her, the one whi
just before the transformation of a child into a woman.
a witness to that change in her whole being, in the innocent
wonder, the restless imagination; I was the first to notice that
sudden tenderness in her glance, the ring of uncertainty in her
voice, and—oh, what a fool! oh, superfluous man!—for a whole
week I was not ashamed to suppose that I, I was the reason for
this change.

This is how it happened.

We walked for quite a long time, right up to evening, and
spoke very little. Like all inexperienced lovers, I remained silent,
while she probably had nothing to say to me; but she seemed to
have something on her mind and shook her head in an odd way,
thoughtfully biting on a leaf she had plucked. Now and then she
would rush ahead, as if she were after something . . . and then she
would suddenly stop and wait for me, looking all around with
raised eyebrows and an absent-minded smile. On the previous
evening we had read *The Prisoner of the Caucasus* together. She
had listened to me with such eagerness, resting her face in both
hands and leaning her bosom against the table! I tried to talk about
our reading from the evening before; she blushed, asked me
whether I had given the bullfinch some birdseed before we left,
started to sing some tune in a loud voice, and then suddenly
stopped.

On one side the grove ended at a rather steep, high cliff; a
small, winding river was flowing down below, and on the other side
of it, stretching into the distance and beyond, were endless meadows, now slightly swelling like waves, now stretching out flat like
a tablecloth, interrupted here and there by ravines. Liza and I were
the first to come to this edge of the grove; Biz'menkov stayed

behind with her mother. We emerged from the grove and stopped, both of us automatically squinting our eyes: directly in front of us, in the midst of a luminous haze, a huge, crimson sun was setting. Half the sky was aglow and flaming; red rays slanted across the meadows, giving even the shady sides of the ravines a scarlet shine. They lay over the river like fiery lead wherever it was not hidden by overhanging bushes; they seemed to rest against the breast of ravine and grove. We stood there, steeped in the burning radiance. I do not have the powers to impart all the passionate solemnity of that scene. It is said that some who are blind picture the color red as the sound of a trumpet; I do not know to what extent this comparison is justified, but there was actually a kind of summons calling out from that flaming gold of the evening air, from the crimson glow of earth and sky.

I cried out with joy and immediately turned to Liza. She was looking directly into the sun. I remember the glare of the sunset was reflected in her eyes in tiny, flaming spots. She was truly struck by it all and deeply moved. She made no reply to my outburst; she stood quite still for a long time and then hung her head. . . . I stretched out my hand to her; she turned away from me and suddenly burst into tears. I looked at her with a secret, almost joyful surprise. . . .

Biz'menkov's voice rang out a couple of steps behind us. Liza quickly wiped away her tears and looked at me with an indecisive smile. Mme Ozhogin emerged from the grove leaning on the arm of her fair-haired escort; each of them took turns admiring the view. The old woman asked Liza about something; I remember a shudder went through me like a reflex when I heard the sound of her daughter's broken voice, like cracked glass, as she answered.

Meanwhile the sun had gone down, and the glow of twilight was beginning to fade. We went back. Once again I gave Liza my

arm. It was still light in the grove, and I could clearly m
the details of her features. Something was troubling her
did not raise her eyes. The flush that had spread all over
had not gone away: it was as though she were standing in the rays
of the setting sun. . . . Her arm was barely touching mine. For a
long time I could not say anything, so hard was my heart pounding
inside of me. The image of a carriage flashed from out of the
distance and through the trees; the coachman was leisurely driving
over the loose sand of the road to meet us.

"Lizaveta Kirillovna," I spoke at last, "why were you crying?"

"I don't know," she answered after a brief silence, looking at
me with her gentle eyes, still wet with tears—it seemed to me that
the look in those eyes had changed—and then she again fell silent.

"I see that you have a love for nature . . . ," I went on. It was
not at all what I wanted to say; indeed, my tongue was hardly able
to stammer its way through this last phrase. She shook her head.
I could not say anything more. . . . I was waiting for something
. . . not a confession, God knows, but a trusting glance, a question.
. . . But Liza stared at the ground and remained silent. Half aloud
I repeated once more, "Why?" and received no answer. I could
see that she was beginning to feel awkward, almost ashamed.

A quarter of an hour later we were all sitting in the carriage
on our way back to town. The horses were moving at a brisk trot;
we quickly whisked our way through the humid air that was now
growing dark. I suddenly began to talk without stopping, first
addressing Biz'menkov and then Mme Ozhogin, without looking at Liza; but I could see that as she sat in the corner of the carriage, her eyes never once rested on me. Once we got home she suddenly recovered, but she did not want to read and soon went off
to bed. That rupture I spoke of before had taken place within her. She was no longer a little girl, and like myself, she had

33

begun to await . . . something. She did not have to wait long.

That night I returned to my room in a state of utter enchantment. The uncertainty that had arisen in me, which was not exactly a foreboding or a suspicion, disappeared; I took the sudden awkwardness in Liza's behavior toward me to be maidenly modesty, shyness. . . . Had I not read a thousand times in countless works that the first appearance of love always disturbs and frightens a young girl? I felt so very happy, and I was already putting together various plans in my mind. . . .

If at that time someone had whispered in my ear, "You are deceiving yourself, my friend! There is nothing of the sort in store for you, dear fellow: you are doomed to die alone in a dirty little house under the unbearable mutterings of an old peasant woman who can hardly wait for you to die so she can sell your boots for a song. . . ."

Yes, like a certain Russian philosopher, one cannot help asking, "How can you know what you do not know?" Until tomorrow.

March 25. A white winter day.

After reading over what I wrote yesterday, I very nearly tore up the whole notebook. My narrative style strikes me as too wordy, too sticky-sweet. But since there is not a trace of joy in the memories I have left of that period in my life—except for that peculiar joy which Lermontov* had in mind when he said it is a glad and painful thing to disturb the sores of an old wound—why, then, shouldn't I indulge myself? But one must draw the line

*M. Yu. Lermontov (1814–41) was an author whom Turgenev admired a great deal; the character Pechorin of Lermontov's *A Hero of Our Times* shares some characteristics with Chulkaturin.

IVAN TURGENEV

somewhere. So I shall proceed without being too maudlin.

For a whole week after that stroll outside of town my situation did not improve in the least, although the change in Liza became more noticeable with the passing of each day. As I said before, I looked upon this change in a way that was most favorable for me. . . . The unhappiness of people who are lonely and shy—shy out of egoism—lies precisely in the fact that even though they have eyes which stare wide open, they either see nothing or see everything in a false light, as if they were looking through tinted glasses. Their observations, indeed their very thoughts, get in their way with every step they take.

When we were first getting acquainted, Liza treated me with trust and openness, like a child; there even might have been a simple, childlike devotion in her feelings toward me. . . . But after that strange and all but sudden crisis had taken place within her, she went through a brief period of confusion and then began to feel uneasy whenever I was around her; she would turn away from me, as though against her own will, and grow sad and pensive. . . . She was expecting . . . what? She herself did not know . . . while I . . . as I have already indicated, I was glad about the change she had gone through. . . . As God is my witness, I practically swooned, as they say, from ecstasy. I am ready to admit, however, that anyone else in my position might have also been deceived. . . . Is there anyone in whom there is no self-centeredness? Needless to say, all this became clear to me only with the passage of time, only after I was forced to lower my injured wings, which were not all that strong anyway.

The misunderstanding that had arisen between Liza and me lasted a whole week—and there is nothing surprising about that: I have been a witness to misunderstandings that have lasted for years and years. And who indeed is to say that truth is the only reality? A lie may cling to life just as tightly as the truth, if not more so. I remember, in fact, that even in the course of that week now and then some worm would stir within me. . . . But I shall say again that someone like myself, a lonely man, is just as incapable of seeing what is happening inside of him as he is of seeing what is taking place right before his eyes. Not only that; one may well ask: Is love really a natural feeling? Is it really man's nature to love? Love is a disease; and there is no law written for a disease. What if my heart did contract so painfully at times? After all, everything inside me was turned upside down. How is a person to know under such circumstances what is right and what is wrong, where the causes lie, and what the significance of every little sensation might be?

Be that as it may, all these misunderstandings, forebodings, and hopes were resolved in the following manner.

One day—it was in the morning, almost noon—before I could step into Mr. Ozhogin's anteroom, I heard an unfamiliar, resonant voice coming from the drawing room. The door flew open, and at the threshold next to the master of the house stood a tall, well-built man of around twenty-five; he quickly slipped on a military overcoat which had been lying on a counter, said a very friendly good-bye to Kirilla Matveich, casually touched his cap as he walked past me, and disappeared with a clink of his spurs.

"Who's that?" I asked Ozhogin.

"Prince N——," he told me with a troubled look on his face. "He's been sent from Petersburg to enlist recruits." Then, annoyed, he continued, "Where is everybody, anyway? There was no one here to help him on with his overcoat."

We went into the drawing room.

"Has he been in town long?" I asked.

"Since yesterday evening, I'm told. I offered him a room in my house, but he declined. He does seem to be a very nice young man, though."

"Was he with you long?"

"About an hour. He asked me to introduce him to my wife, Olimpiada Nikitichna."

"And did you introduce him?"

"Of course."

"And what about Lizaveta Kirillovna . . . ?"

"He was introduced to her too, of course."

I remained silent for a while and then asked, "Do you know if he plans to be here long?"

"Yes, I think he'll have to stay for a couple of weeks or more."

Then Kirilla Matveich ran off to get dressed.

I paced up and down the drawing room several times. I do not recall that Prince N—— made any special impression on me at that time, except for that feeling of hostility which usually comes over us when a new face enters our domestic circle. Perhaps mixed in with that feeling was a timid, obscure Muscovite's jealousy over the brilliant officer from Petersburg.

"The Prince," I thought to myself, "is a swagger stick from the capital; he's bound to look down on us. . . ."

I had not seen him for more than a minute, but it was long enough to notice that he was handsome, clever, and uninhibited.

After pacing around the drawing room for a while, I stopped finally in front of the mirror, pulled a small comb from my pocket, and gave my hair a casual, picturesque look; then, as sometimes happens, I suddenly became engrossed in the contemplation of my own face. I remember carefully focusing my attention on my nose; I was deriving no particular satisfaction from the soft, undefined contours of that appendage—when suddenly, in the dark depths of the tilted glass that reflected almost the entire room, the door opened and there was Liza's shapely figure. I do not know why I failed to move or why I continued to hold the same expression on my face.

Liza stretched her head forward and took a close look at me; she raised her eyebrows, bit her lips, and held her breath, like someone who was glad she had not been seen; then she carefully stepped back and started to close the door quietly behind her. The door creaked slightly. Liza jumped and then froze at the spot. . . . I did not make a move. . . . She pulled at the doorknob again and then disappeared.

There was no doubt about it: the expression on Liza's face as she was looking at me was one which revealed nothing but a desire to get out of there as quickly as possible and avoid an unpleasant encounter; that flash of gratification I detected in her eyes when she thought she had actually succeeded in slipping away unnoticed demonstrated to me all too clearly that this young woman was not in love with me. For a long time, a very long time, I could not tear my gaze from the mute, motionless door which once again appeared as a white spot in the depths of the mirror. I made an effort to smile at my own drawn figure; I hung my head, went home, and threw myself on the divan. I was crushed as I had never been crushed before, so crushed that I could not weep . . . and what indeed was there to weep about?

"Can it be?" I kept repeating over and over, lying on my back like a dead man, my hands folded over my chest. "Can it be . . . ?"

Tell me, how do you like that "Can it be?"

March 26. A thaw.

When on the following day, after long hesitations and inward fits and starts, I walked in to the familiar Ozhogin parlor, I was no longer the same man whom they had come to know over the past three weeks. All my old ways and mannerisms, those habits which I had begun to leave behind me under the influence of that new emotion I had felt, suddenly came back again and took possession of me like masters returning to to their house. Generally people like me are guided not so much by positive facts as by their own impressions; only yesterday I had been dreaming of "the joys of mutual love," while today I had no doubts whatsoever about my own "unhappiness" and was in a state of utter despair, even though I myself was unable to find any rational grounds for my despair. Nor could I be jealous of Prince N——; no matter what good qualities he may have had, his mere appearance could not have been enough to erase in one stroke Liza's inclination toward me. . . .

But wait a minute. Did such a liking for me even exist? I thought back to the past. "What about the stroll in the wood?" I asked myself. "And the expression on her face in the mirror? But," I went on, "perhaps the stroll in the wood was. . . . Oh, good God, what a worthless creature I am!" This I finally exclaimed out loud. Such were the half-articulated, half-thought ideas that returned to me a thousand times, spinning around in my head like a monotonous whirlwind. I repeat: I returned to the Ozhogin home as the same mistrustful, suspicious, withdrawn person I had been since my childhood.

I found the whole family sitting in the parlor; Biz'menkov was there too, seated in a corner. Everyone seemed to be in good spirits: Ozhogin in particular was positively beaming, and his first words were to let me know that yesterday Prince N——— had spent the whole evening with them. Liza offered me a quiet greeting.

"Well," I said to myself, "now I see why you are in such a good mood."

To tell the truth, I was puzzled by the Prince's second visit. I had not expected that. Generally, people like me expect everything in the world except the very thing that must happen according to the natural flow of events. I sulked and assumed the air of an insulted but magnanimous man; I wanted to punish Liza for the disgrace she caused me. From all this it may be concluded that I had not yet sunk completely into despair after all. It is said that when you are loved, it may even be useful in some cases to torment the one you adore. But in my position this would be unspeakably stupid: Liza, in a most innocent way, paid no attention to me. Mme Ozhogin was the only one who noticed my solemn reticence, and she made solicitous inquiries about my health. I, of course, told her with a bitter smile that I was quite healthy, thank God. Ozhogin continued to elaborate on the subject of his guest; but once he saw that I was answering his remarks unwillingly, he turned to Biz'menkov, who was listening to him very attentively, when suddenly a man came in and announced the arrival of Prince N———. The master of the house jumped up and ran out to meet him; immediately I cast an eagle eye in Liza's direction and saw her blush with pleasure and begin fidgeting around in her chair. The Prince came in, perfumed, cheerful, friendly. . . .

Since I am not composing a story to win the sympathy of the reader but am simply writing for my own pleasure, there is no need for me to resort to the usual artificial devices employed by men of letters. So right now, without any further delay, I shall say that Liza was passionately in love with the Prince from the first day she met him, and he was in love with her—partly because he had nothing better to do, partly because he was used to having women flock around him, but also partly because Liza was a very charming creature. There was nothing particularly surprising about the fact that they loved each other. He probably had not expected to find such a pearl in such a dirty little shell (I am referring to the Godforsaken town of O——); and up till that time, even in her dreams, she had never seen anyone that even remotely resembled this dashing, intelligent, captivating aristocrat.

After the preliminary greetings Ozhogin introduced me to the Prince, who was very polite toward me. In fact, he was very polite toward everyone, and despite the incommensurable distance that separated him from our obscure rural circle, he knew not only how to keep from making anyone feel uneasy but how to make it seem as if he were our equal, as if it were by mere chance that he happened to live in St. Petersburg.

That first evening . . . oh, that first evening! In the happy days of our childhood teachers used to present us with the example of the courageous endurance of the young Lacedaemonian who had stolen a fox and had hidden it under his cloak; without once crying out, he allowed the fox to devour all his entrails, thus showing that he preferred death itself to dishonor. . . . I can find no better comparison to express my unutterable sufferings in the course of that evening, when for the first time I saw the Prince at Liza's side. My constant, constrained smile, my agonizing perceptiveness, my stupid silence, my sad and vain longing to get out of there—in its way all this must have been extremely noticeable. There was more than one fox eating away at my insides: jealousy, envy, a feeling of worthlessness, and impotent rage were tearing me apart. I could not help admitting that the Prince was actually a very amiable young man. . . . I devoured him with my eyes; I believe I truly forgot to wink as I was looking at him. Although he did not talk only to Liza, she was, of course, the sole topic of his conversation. I must have been terribly boring to him. . . . He probably guessed very quickly that he was dealing with a discarded lover, but because he took pity on me and had a deep sense of my utter harmlessness, he treated me with unusual gentleness. You can imagine what an insult this was to me!

I remember that in the course of the evening I tried to make up for the way I had been acting; I (do not laugh at me, whoever you are, whose eyes happen to fall upon these lines, especially since this was my last dream) . . . as God is my witness, I suddenly imagined, in the middle of my various torments, that Liza wanted to punish me for my arrogant coldness at the beginning of my visit, that she was angry with me and was flirting with the Prince only because she was annoyed at me. . . .

Seizing an opportune moment, I went up to her with a meek but affectionate smile and mumbled, "Enough, forgive me. . . . I do not ask it, though, because I am afraid."

And suddenly, without waiting for her to answer, my face took on an unusually animated and impudent expression; I smiled ironically, threw my hand up over my head toward the ceiling (I remember wanting to adjust my neckerchief), and was even about to turn around on one foot, as if to say, "That's all there is to that. I'm in good spirits now; let everyone be in good spirits." But I did not turn around like that, since I have this unnatural stiffness in my knees and was afraid of falling down. . . . Liza did not understand me in the least; she looked me in the face with surprise, smiled hurriedly, as if wanting to get rid of me as quickly as possible, and then went over to the Prince again. No matter how blind and deaf I might have been, I could not help admitting to myself that she was not a bit angry or annoyed at me; she simply had not given me any thought. It was a decisive blow. The last of my hopes came tumbling down with a crash, just as a block of ice beaten down by the spring sun suddenly crumbles into tiny fragments. I had been utterly defeated on the first assault, and like the Prussians at Jena, in one day I lost everything in a single stroke. No, she was not angry with me! . . .

Alas, on the contrary! I could see that she herself was being undermined, as though a wave were rolling over her. Like a young sapling who has already half deserted the bank, she was eagerly leaning out over the rushing torrent, ready to offer it once and for all both her first spring blossom and her entire life. Anyone who may have had the chance to witness such a passion has lived through some bitter moments, if he himself loved without being loved in return. I shall always remember the consuming kindness, the tender gaiety, the innocent selflessness, the still-childlike and yet womanly glance, the happy smile that burst forth like a flower in bloom and never abandoned those half-parted lips and blushing cheeks. . . . Everything that Liza had only vaguely anticipated during our stroll in the grove was now taking place—and giving herself over to love completely, she had at once brightened up and calmed down, like a new wine that has ceased to ferment because its time has come. . . .

I had the patience to sit out that first evening and the evenings which followed . . . all to the bitter end! There was not a shred of hope left for me. Liza and the Prince grew more and more attached to each other with the passing of each day. . . . But I had lost absolutely all sense of my own dignity and could not tear myself away from the spectacle of my unhappiness. I remember that one day I tried not to go there; that morning I had given myself my word of honor that I would stay home—and at eight o'clock in the evening (I usually went out at seven) I jumped up like a madman, put on my hat, and ran, panting, to Kirilla Matveich's parlor.

My position was extremely awkward; I maintained a stubborn silence, and sometimes for days on end I would never utter a sound. As I have already said, I have never been known for my eloquence; but now everything that went through my mind seemed to vanish into thin air whenever I was around the Prince, and I remained as poor as a church mouse. Moreover, as I slowly pondered everything I had observed or noted in the course of the preceding day, I would privately force my unhappy brain to work so hard that when I returned to the Ozhogin home I scarcely had enough strength left to go on with my observations. They spared me as if I were an invalid; I saw that.

Every morning I would come to a new and final decision which, for the most part, had been torturously hatched out in the course of a sleepless night: I was all set to offer Liza some explanation, to give her some friendly advice . . . but whenever I happened to be alone with her, my tongue would suddenly quit working, as if it were frozen stiff, and both of us would sit there in silence, waiting for a third person to come along. There were times when I wanted to run away once and for all just so I could leave behind a letter full of reproach, and one day I actually started the letter, but I had not yet lost all sense of fairness: I realized that I had no right to reproach anyone for anything, and I threw my note into the fire. On other occasions I would suddenly and generously offer myself in sacrifice, bestowing upon Liza my blessing for happiness in love and giving the Prince a gentle, warmhearted smile from my corner. Yet the callous lovers not only failed to thank me for my sacrifice but did not even notice it and apparently had no need for my blessings or for my smiles. . . . Then, full of spite, I would switch over to a completely opposite frame of mind. Throwing my cape over my shoulders in a Spanish style, I gave myself my word that I would sneak up from around some corner and slit my happy rival's throat; with savage relish I pictured Liza's despair. . . . But in the first place, there were not very many corners in the town of O—— that would do; and in the second place, a wooden fence, a street light, a policeman in the distance. . . . No! Such corners were more suited for peddling bagels than for shedding human blood.

I must confess that among other means of seeking deliverance, as I vaguely referred to it in my conversations with myself, I thought of appealing to Ozhogin himself. . . . of calling that noble gentleman's attention to the dangerous position his daughter was in, pointing out to him the grim consequences of her reckless behavior. . . . One day I spoke to him about this delicate matter, but I chose my words so cleverly and obscurely that he listened and listened for a long time—and then suddenly, like a man waking up from a sound sleep, he ran the palm of his hand over his face hard and fast, without even sparing his nose, snorted, and walked away from me.

Needless to say, when I had reached this decision, I assured myself that I was acting out of the most unselfish motives, that I wanted what was best for everyone, that I was fulfilling the duty of a friend of the family. . . . But I dare say that even if Kirilla Matveich had not cut short my outpourings, I still would not have had the courage to finish my monologue. Sometimes, taking on the solemn air of an ancient sage, I would presume to weigh the merits of the Prince; at other times I would console myself with the hope that it was all just a passing fancy, that Liza would realize her love was not true love . . . oh, no! In short, I do not know of

45

a single thought which I did not labor over at that time. I admit quite openly that there was, however, one remedy which never entered my mind, namely taking my own life. Why this never occurred to me, I do not know. . . . Perhaps even then I already had some foreboding that I did not have long to live.

Of course, under such unfavorable circumstances my behavior, the way I acted around people, was more unnatural and constrained than ever. Even Mme Ozhogin—that feeble-minded creature—began to shun me and did not know what to think of me. Biz'menkov, who was always polite and ready to be of service, avoided me. At the time I thought that in him I had already found a companion and that he too was in love with Liza. But he never responded to my hints and was generally reluctant to talk to me. The Prince was very friendly toward him; one might even say that the Prince respected him. Neither Biz'menkov nor I interfered with Liza and the Prince. But he did not avoid being around them, as I did; he did not moan and groan or take on the air of a sacrificial victim—and he gladly joined them whenever they wanted him to. It is true that on such occasions he was not in a particularly joking mood, but even before that there had always been a quiet aspect to his humor.

This went on for about two weeks. The Prince was not only handsome and intelligent; he played the piano, sang, drew fairly well, and knew how to tell a good story. His anecdotes, drawn from the highest circles of society in the capital, always made a striking impression on his listeners, an impression which was all the more striking since he did not seem to attach any particular importance to the stories he told. . . .

The result of the Prince's unaffected subterfuge, if you want to call it that, was that in the course of his brief stay in the town of O—— he absolutely charmed the whole of the local society. It is always very easy for a man from the highest circles to charm us steppe dwellers. The Prince's frequent visits to the Ozhogin home (he spent his evenings at their house), of course, aroused the envy of the rest of the gentry and other officials; but like a clever man of the world, the Prince did not leave a single one of them out. He called on all of them, spoke an endearing word or two to all the fine ladies and their daughters, and allowed himself to be fed terribly rich food and treated to wretched wines with grand names —in a word, he conducted himself admirably, cautiously, and cleverly. Prince N—— was generally a man of cheerful disposition, sociable, amiable by inclination as well as by calculation; how could he help being a complete success in everything he did?

From the moment of his arrival everyone in the house thought the time was flying by all too quickly; everything went beautifully. Although he pretended not to notice anything, old Ozhogin must have been secretly rubbing his hands together at the thought of having such a son-in-law; the Prince himself was handling everything very calmly and properly, when suddenly a certain unexpected incident. . . .

But I shall leave that for tomorrow. Right now I am tired. Even as I stand at the edge of the grave, these memories still bother me. Today Terent'evna thought my snout was starting to look even more pointed; they say that is a bad sign.

March 27. The thaw continues.

Everything went along as described above; Liza and the Prince were in love with each other, and old Ozhogin was waiting to see what would come of it; Biz'menkov continued to hang around—

that's about all that can be said of him. I was floundering like a
fish on ice and was keeping watch as best I could—I remember
that at the time I appointed myself the task of at least preventing
Liza from perishing in the snares of her seducer, and as a result,
I had begun to pay particular attention to the chambermaids and
to the fatal "back door." On the other hand, however, I sometimes
dreamt all through the night about the touching generosity with
which, in the course of time, I would extend my hand to the
deluded victim and say to her, "That treacherous man has betrayed you; but I am your faithful friend . . . let us forget the past
and be happy!" Then suddenly a joyful bit of news spread throughout the town: the local Marshal of Nobility was planning to give
a grand ball in honor of our esteemed visitor at his own Gornostaevka estate, which was also known as Gubnyakova.

All the people of position and power in the town of O——
received invitations, beginning with the chief of police and ending
with the apothecary, a remarkably pimple-faced German with
cruel pretensions of knowing how to speak Russian fluently; as a
result he was continually using strong expressions that were completely out of place, such as "Vell, I vill be dahmned alzugether,
if I don't feel today an alzugether goot fellow. . . ." Frantic
preparations in keeping with the occasion were under way. One
cosmetic shop sold sixteen jars of pomade with the inscription "à
la jasmin," spelled with a hard sign after the *n*. * The young ladies
outfitted themselves with stiff gowns that were painfully tight
around the middle and had sashes draped from the waist; the
mothers placed various sorts of outlandish decorations on their
own heads, under the pretext that they were hats; the busy fathers
ran themselves ragged, as the saying goes. . . .

*The hard sign is a letter of the Russian alphabet, here added at the end of the
French word for "jasmine."

IVAN TURGENEV

The long-awaited day finally arrived. I was among those who were invited. Gornostaevka was about nine versts outside of town. Kirilla Matveich offered me a ride in his carriage; but I declined . . . just as a child who wants to really get even with his parents for their punishing him might refuse to eat his favorite foods at the dinner table. Besides, I felt that my presence would bother Liza. Biz'menkov took my place. The Prince went in his own coach, while I rode in a miserable little cart that I had hired at an exorbitant rate for the festive occasion.

I am not going to describe the ball. Everything about it was as usual: the musicians with unbelievably phony-looking horns in the gallery, the confused landowners with old families, ice cream the color of lilacs, slimy orgeat, men with worn-out boots and knitted cotton gloves, provincial lions with convulsively distorted faces, and so on, and so forth. And the whole of this little world revolved around its sun—around the Prince. Lost in the crowd, unnoticed even by the forty-eight-year-old maidens with red pimples on their foreheads and blue flowers at their temples, I was constantly looking now at Liza, now at the Prince. She was very nicely dressed and quite beautiful that evening. They danced with each other only twice (true, he danced the mazurka with her!), but to *me* at least it seemed that there was some sort of mysterious exchange continually going on between them. Even when he was not looking at her or talking to her, he seemed to be constantly addressing her, and her alone; he was handsome and brilliant and friendly with others—for her sake alone. She was evidently conscious of the fact that she was the queen of the ball—and loved by all: her face beamed at once with childlike joy and innocent pride, and then it would suddenly light up with another, deeper feeling. She radiated happiness. I took note of all this. . . . It was not the first time I had had occasion to observe them. . . . In the

49

beginning it was all very painful to me, then I seemed to be moved by it, and finally it infuriated me. I suddenly felt remarkably malicious, and I remember taking an unusual delight in this new sensation; it even produced in me a certain respect for myself.

"Let's show them that we aren't finished yet," I said to myself.

When the first sounds calling everyone to the mazurka began to ring out, I calmly looked around and walked up in a cool and easy manner to a long-faced young lady with a shiny red nose, a mouth that looked like it had been unbuttoned, and a wiry neck that reminded me of the neck on a double bass—I walked up to her, dryly clicked my heels together, and invited her to dance. She was wearing a pink gown which looked as if it had recently started to fade but had not yet lost all its color; some object that resembled a dismal, discolored fly was dangling above her head on the end of a very thick brass spring; indeed, this young woman generally and thoroughly reeked, if one may use that expression, with the sour smell of boredom and an ancient lack of success. Since the very beginning of the evening she had not budged from her seat: no one had thought of asking her to dance. After having failed to find any other partner, one blond, sixteen-year-old boy had started to approach this young lady and had even taken a step in her direction, when he took another look, had a second thought, and promptly hid himself in the crowd. You can imagine the joyful surprise with which she accepted my invitation!

I solemnly led her all the way across the ballroom, found two chairs, and sat down with her in the mazurka circle; we were the tenth couple, seated almost directly across from the Prince, who, of course, had been given the first position. As I have already said, the Prince danced with Liza. Neither my partner nor I was over-whelmed with invitations to dance; so we had plenty of time to talk. To tell the truth, my partner did not appear to be noted for her ability to arrange her words into coherent speech: instead, she used her mouth to form a smile that was turned downward in a strange way, something I had not noticed until then. At the same time her eyes were turned upward, as though some invisible force were stretching out her face; but I had no need of her eloquence. I was in a malicious mood, and, fortunately, my partner did not instill me with timidity. I started criticizing everyone and everything in the world, placing particular emphasis on the upstarts from the capital and the Petersburg fops, until I finally became so angry that my lady gradually quit smiling, and instead of turning her eyes upward, she suddenly—it must have been from sheer amazement—began to look cross-eyed in a very odd manner, as if she had noticed for the first time that she had a nose. And the man sitting next to me, one of those lions I mentioned before, glanced at me more than once and even turned to face me with the look of an actor on a stage who had just awakened in the middle of some unknown land, as though he wanted to say, "Are you still at it?"

However, while I was singing like a nightingale, as the saying goes, I still continued to watch Liza and the Prince. They were constantly being invited to dance; but I suffered less when they were both dancing and even when they were sitting together and talking to one another, smiling that gentle smile that never wants to leave the faces of happy lovers—even then I was not tormented quite so much. But when Liza was fluttering about the ballroom with some dashing dandy, while the Prince sat there with her blue gauze scarf over his knees, thoughtfully following her with his eyes, as if he were admiring his latest conquest—then, oh, then I suffered unbearable agonies and let out such embittered, malicious remarks that the pupils of my partner's eyes were both rivted to her nose!

Meanwhile the mazurka was coming to an end. . . . They began doing the figure known as "la confidente." In this figure the lady takes a seat in the middle of the circle, chooses another lady for her confidante, and whispers in her ear the name of the gentleman with whom she wishes to dance; one of the male partners leads the dancers up to her one at a time, and the confidante turns them down until they finally come to the happy fellow whose name had been whispered. Liza sat down in the center of the circle and selected for her confidante the host's daughter, one of those young ladies of whom it may be said, "She's nothing to write home about." As Liza's partner, the Prince set out to search for the man she had chosen. He introduced ten or so young men to no avail (the host's daughter turned them all down with a pleasant smile), and at last he came to me. Something extraordinary happened inside of me at that moment: I seemed to wince with my whole body and tried to refuse, yet I got up and went with him. The Prince led me up to Liza. . . . She did not even look at me; the host's daughter shook her head no, and the Prince, probably prompted by the gooselike expression on my face, turned to me and gave me a deep bow. This mocking gesture, the rejection which my triumphant rival handed to me, his casual smile, Liza's indifferent lack of attention—all of it enraged me. . . .

I went up to the Prince and whispered with incensed anger, "I think you are permitting yourself to laugh at me!"

The Prince stared at me with a look of contemptuous surprise, once again took me by the hand, and, acting as though he were going to take me back to my seat, replied, "I?"

"Yes, you!" I continued under my breath, obeying him nonetheless—that is, going with him back to my seat. "You! But I do not intend to let some frivolous Petersburg upstart. . . ."

The Prince gave me a calm, ironic, almost condescending

smile, squeezed my hand, and said in a low voice, "I understand you completely, but this is not the place; we shall discuss it later." Then he turned away from me, went over to Biz'menkov, and led him up to Liza. This pale, petty official turned out to be the one whom she had chosen. Liza got up to meet him.

Sitting next to my partner with the doleful fly on her head, I felt almost like a hero. My heart was pounding rapidly, my chest swelled nobly under my starched shirt front, I was breathing deep and fast—and all of a sudden I gave the lion at my side such a magnificent look that the leg he had turned toward me started to tremble all on its own. Having disposed of this man, I ran my eyes over the entire circle of dancers. . . . It appeared to me that two or three of the gentlemen were looking in my direction not without some astonishment; but on the whole, my exchange with the Prince had gone unnoticed. My rival was already sitting in his chair, perfectly composed, with his former smile on his face. Biz'menkov brought Liza back to her seat. She gave him a friendly nod and then turned to face the Prince with what seemed to me to be a look of some anxiety; but he replied to her with a laugh, gracefully waved his hand, and must have said something very pleasant to her, for she blushed with pleasure, glanced down, and then looked up at him in tender reproach.

The heroic attitude that had suddenly come over me did not fade away until the end of the mazurka; but I quit cracking jokes and stopped "criticizing"; instead, I simply gave my partner a dark, stern look from time to time. Apparently, she was beginning to be afraid of me: her speech was reduced to absolute stuttering, and she was winking and blinking incessantly when I took her back to the natural stronghold of her mother, a very fat woman who wore a reddish toque on her head. . . . Having handed over the intimidated young lady, which was the only proper thing to do,

I went to the window, clasped my hands together, and began to wait to see what would happen. I waited a rather long time. All the while, the Prince was surrounded by the host—and I do mean surrounded, just as England is surrounded by the sea—not to mention other members of the Marshal of Nobility's family and various guests; to be sure, he could not very well approach such an insignificant man as myself and enter into conversation without arousing the gaping astonishment of everyone there. I remember that it was precisely my insignificance which at the time filled me with delight.

"You had better watch your step," I thought, as I watched him politely turn from one distinguished person to the next, each of whom was trying to obtain the honor of being noticed by him, if only for a "fleeting moment," as the poets say. "You had better watch your step, my friend. . . . You will come to me sooner or later—after all, I have insulted you."

After tactfully getting rid of the crowd of his admirers, the Prince finally walked past me, glancing not exactly at the window, nor exactly at my hair; he started to turn away, when he suddenly stopped, as if he had just remembered something.

"Ah, yes," he said, facing me with a smile. "It seems that I have a little matter to settle with you."

Two landowners, among the most persistent of those who were stubbornly following the Prince around, probably took the "little matter" to be something pertaining to government service and stepped back a couple of respectful paces. The Prince took me by the arm and led me aside. My heart was pounding against my chest.

"It seems that you," he began, drawing out the word "you" and staring at my chin with a contemptuous expression which, in a curious way, made his face look all the more refreshing and handsome, "you made some insolent remark to me."

"I said what I thought," I answered, raising my voice.

"Shh . . . not so loud," he commented. "Decent people do not shout. Perhaps you would like to fight with me."

"That is up to you," I replied, straightening myself up.

"I'm afraid I shall have to call you out," he said casually, "if you do not take back what you said. . . ."

"I have absolutely no intention of taking anything back," I declared with pride.

"Are you quite sure?" he asked, not without a mocking grin. "In that case," he continued after a brief pause, "I shall have the honor of sending my second to you in the morning."

"Very well, sir," I rejoined in the most indifferent tone I could manage.

The Prince bowed slightly.

"I cannot forbid you to take me for a frivolous man," he added, arrogantly narrowing his eyes, "but a Prince N—— cannot be considered an upstart. Until we meet again, Mr. . . . Mr. Shtukaturin."*

He quickly turned his back on me and went over again to the host, who was already starting to get upset.

Mr. Shtukaturin! . . . My name is Chulkaturin. . . . I was unable to come up with anything to say in response to this final insult and could only stare after him in blinding rage. "Until tomorrow," I whispered through clenched teeth. Then I immediately sought out an officer I knew, Captain Koloberdyaev of the Uhlans,† who

*The name *Shtukaturin* means "plasterer," so its use by the Prince is an insulting play on Chulkaturin's name and social standing. The root word *shtuka* may also be significant here, since it may be used to refer to some trivial thing or object or even a practical joke.

†The Uhlans were a light-cavalry group originally modeled after the Tartar lancers.

was an awful carouser and a good fellow; I briefly told him about my quarrel with the Prince and asked him to be my second. He, of course, agreed right away, and I set off for home.

I could not get to sleep the whole night—from excitement, not from cowardice. I am no coward. I hardly even gave a thought to the possibility which now confronted me of losing my life, that prospect which the Germans regard as the greatest good on earth. I thought only of Liza, of my dead hopes, of what I ought to do.

"Should I try to kill the Prince?" I asked myself, and certainly I wanted to kill him, not out of vengeance but for the sake of Liza's well-being. "But she could never survive such a blow," I continued. "No, it would be better to allow him to kill me!"

I admit that I also took some pleasure in supposing that I, an obscure man from the country, had forced such an important figure to fight a duel with me.

Dawn found me engrossed in these reflections; Koloberdyaev showed up not long after sunrise.

"So where is the Prince's second?" he asked me, noisily entering my bedroom.

"Take it easy," I answered, somewhat annoyed. "It's only seven o'clock in the morning; the Prince is probably still asleep."

"In that case," the irrepressible cavalry captain retorted, "order me some tea. Last night left me with a headache. . . . I haven't even changed clothes. But," he added with a yawn, "I seldom change clothes anyway."

He got his tea. He drank six glasses of it with rum, smoked four pipes, told me that on the previous day he had bought a horse for a pittance from a coachman who had given up on it and that he planned to break the animal by tying its front legs together—and then he fell asleep in his clothes on the divan with a pipe stuck in his mouth. I got up and put my papers in order. I came across a note of invitation from Liza, the only note I had ever received from her; I started to slip it into my shirt next to my breast, but I changed my mind and tossed it into a box. Koloberdyaev was snoring softly, his head hanging over the leather cushion. . . . I remember looking for a long time at his disheveled, bold, carefree, and good-natured face.

At ten o'clock my servant announced the arrival of Biz'men-kov. The Prince had chosen him as his second!

Together we roused the captain from his sound sleep. He rose, looked at us through owlish eyes, and in a hoarse voice asked for some vodka; then he regained his senses, exchanged greetings with Biz'menkov, and the two of them went into the other room for a conference. It did not take the seconds long to finish their consultation. A quarter of an hour later they both came to me in my bedroom; Koloberdyaev informed me that the Prince and I would "fight a duel this afternoon at three o'clock with pistols." I nodded my head in silent agreement. Biz'menkov immediately said his good-byes and left. He looked somewhat pale and seemed to be inwardly agitated, like a man who was not used to doing such things, but he was very polite and cool nevertheless. I felt rather ashamed in front of him and did not dare to look him in the eye.

Koloberdyaev started talking about his horse again. This conversation was very much to my liking. I was afraid he might mention Liza. But my good captain was no scandalmonger; indeed, more than that, he despised all women, referring to them, God knows why, as salad. We had lunch at two o'clock, and at three we were already on the field of action—in the very same birch grove where at one time I had strolled with Liza, just a couple of paces from the cliff.

We were the first to arrive. But we did not have to wait long for the Prince and Biz'menkov. The Prince was, without exaggeration, as fresh as a rose: his dark brown eyes peered out from under the visor of his military cap in an extraordinarily friendly way. He was smoking a small straw cigar, and as soon as he saw Koloberdyaev, he cordially extended his hand to him. He even bowed very graciously to me. I, on the other hand, was feeling pale, and to my profound consternation, my hands were slightly trembling . . . my throat was dry. . . . Until that time I had never fought a duel.

"Oh, God!" I thought. "If only this sneering gentleman does not take my nervousness for timidity!"

Inwardly I packed my nerves off to the devil. But when I finally looked directly into the Prince's face and caught sight of the almost imperceptible smile on his lips, I was once again stricken with rage and then immediately regained control of myself.

Meanwhile our seconds had set up the boundary lines for the duel, measured off the paces, and loaded the pistols. Koloberdyaev took care of most of it; for the most part Biz'menkov just watched. It was a magnificent day—not much different from the day of that unforgettable stroll. As before, the deep blue of the sky could be seen through the gilded green of the leaves. Their rustling seemed to excite me. The Prince continued to puff on his cigar, as he leaned his shoulder against the trunk of a young linden tree. . . .

"Please take your places, gentlemen; we're ready," Koloberdyaev announced at last, handing us the pistols.

The Prince stepped off a few paces, stopped, and, turning his head back over his shoulder, asked me, "And do you still refuse to take back your words?"

I wanted to answer him; but my voice failed me, and I had to be satisfied with a disdainful wave of my hand. The Prince smiled once more and took his position. We began walking toward each other. I raised my pistol and started to take aim at my enemy's chest—at that moment he was truly my enemy—but suddenly the barrel reared up, as if someone had bumped my elbow, and fired. The Prince staggered and lifted his left hand to his left temple— from under his white suede glove a small stream of blood trickled down his cheek. Biz'menkov ran up to him.

"It's nothing," he said, taking off his cap, which now had a hole in it. "If the bullet didn't enter my head, it must be only a scratch."

He calmly pulled a cambric handkerchief from his pocket and laid it on his curls, now wet with blood. I looked at him, dumbfounded, and did not budge from my spot.

"Please go to the barrier!" Koloberdyaev sternly remarked to me.

I obeyed.

"Shall the duel go on?" he added, turning to Biz'menkov.

Biz'menkov gave him no response; but without removing his handkerchief from his wound or even giving himself the satisfaction of tormenting me at the barrier, the Prince answered with a smile, "The duel is over"—and fired into the air. I all but wept with resentment and rage. That man had trampled me into the mud once and for all with his generosity; it was as though he had cut my throat. I wanted to protest, to demand that he fire at me; but he walked up to me and offered me his hand.

"So everything is forgotten between us, okay?" he uttered in a friendly voice.

I looked into his pale face, at the bloodstained handkerchief, and completely flustered, shamed, and annihilated, I pressed his hand. . . .

"Gentlemen!" he added, turning to the seconds. "I trust all this will remain a secret."

"Of course!" Koloberdyaev exclaimed. "But, Prince, allow me. . . ."

And he bound up the Prince's head himself.

As he was walking off, the Prince bowed to me once more; but Biz'menkov did not even look at me. Slain—morally slain—I returned home with Koloberdyaev.

"So what's the matter with you?" the captain asked me. "Calm down; the wound isn't serious. He can go dancing tomorrow if he likes. Or is it that you're sorry you didn't kill him? If that's the case, then you're wrong; he's a good man."

"Why did he spare me?" I muttered at last.

"Oh, so that's it," he calmly retorted. "I swear, these romantics will be the death of me!"

I absolutely refuse to describe the agony I went through in the course of the evening which followed that unhappy duel. My self-respect suffered unspeakably. It was not my conscience that tormented me; no, I was destroyed by the painful awareness of my stupidity.

"I am the one who has dealt myself the final, ultimate blow!" I repeated over and over, pacing about the room with long strides. "The Prince's forgiving me after I had wounded him . . . yes, Liza is now his. Nothing can save her now, nothing can hold her back from the edge of the abyss."

I knew very well that our duel could not be kept a secret, in spite of what the Prince had said; at any rate, it could not be kept a secret from Liza.

"The Prince is not stupid enough to fail to take advantage of it," I whispered in a frenzy.

And yet I was mistaken. The whole town found out about the duel and about the actual reason behind it—the very next day, of course. But the Prince was not the one who had spread the news around; on the contrary, by the time the Prince had shown up to see Liza with his head bandaged and an excuse prepared beforehand, she already knew all about it. . . . Whether Biz'menkov had betrayed me or whether the news had reached her by other means, I cannot say. And, after all, is it really possible to hide anything in a small town? You can well imagine how Liza took it, indeed, how the entire Ozhogin family took it!

As for me, I suddenly became the object of universal indignation and loathing, a monster, an insanely jealous man, and a cannibal. My few acquaintances avoided me as they might avoid a leper. The town authorities went to the Prince and suggested that they should make an example of me and punish me severely; only the urgent and persistent entreaties of the Prince himself averted the calamity that was hanging over my head. This man was fated to annihilate me in every way possible. By his very magnanimity he sealed the lid of my coffin over me.

Needless to say, the Ozhogin house was immediately closed to me. Kirilla Matveich even returned to me an ordinary pencil that I had left there. Actually, he was precisely the one who should not have been angry with me. My "insane" jealousy, as they referred to it throughout the town, defined—brought to light, so to speak —the relationship between Liza and the Prince. The elder Ozhogins themselves, as well as other local people, began to look upon him almost as Liza's fiancé. Such a notion could not, in fact, have been entirely agreeable to the Prince; but he did like Liza very much; moreover, at that time he had not yet obtained his object. . . . With all the tact of a clever and worldly man, he adapted to his new situation and immediately entered into the spirit of his new role, as they say. . . .

But I! . . . As far as I was concerned, as far as my future was concerned, I gave it all up as hopeless. When our sufferings reach the point where they make our whole inner being crack and creak like an overloaded cart, they should no longer seem ridiculous to us. . . . But no! Laughter not only accompanies tears to the end, to exhaustion, to the point where it is impossible to shed any more of them—not at all!—it continues to ring and resound even after the tongue has grown mute and every plaintive outcry has died away. . . . And so, first of all, since I have no intention of appearing ridiculous to myself, and second of all, since I am terribly tired, I shall put off continuing with my story and, God willing, I shall leave the conclusion for tomorrow. . . .

March 29. A light frost;
yesterday there was a thaw.

I did not have the strength to continue with my diary yesterday; like Poprishchin, I spent most of my time lying in bed and chatting with Terent'evna. What a woman she is! Sixty years ago she lost her first fiancé to the plague, she has outlived all her children, she herself is unpardonably old, she drinks tea to her heart's content, she is well fed and has warm clothes; and what do you suppose she spent the whole time talking about yesterday? I had ordered that the cape of an ancient, threadbare livery coat be given to another old woman, who was completely destitute, so she could make it into a jacket (she had been wearing a vest for a jacket); half of it had been eaten away by moths . . . so why shouldn't she have it?

"But it seems to me that since I am your nurse. . . . Oh, dear fellow, it's a sin for you to do that. . . . Aren't I the one who has been taking care of you? . . ." And so on. The merciless old woman absolutely wore me out with her reproaches. But let us return to the story.

And so I suffered like a dog who has had the hind part of his body run over by a wheel. Only then, only after my expulsion from the Ozhogin home, did I find out once and for all how much pleasure a man can derive from the contemplation of his own unhappiness. Oh, people! What a pitiful lot you are! . . . But I am slipping into philosophical remarks. . . .

I spent my days in complete solitude, and it was only in the most roundabout and even base ways that I was able to find out what was going on in the Ozhogin family and what the Prince was up to: my servant struck up an acquaintance with the first cousin once removed of the wife of the Prince's coachman. This relationship made things a little easier for me, and after I had dropped him a few hints and given him a few gifts, my servant was soon able to guess what he was supposed to discuss with his master when he was pulling off his master's boots in the evening. Every once in a while I happened to run into Biz'menkov or the Prince or someone from the Ozhogin family on the street. . . . I exchanged bows with Biz'menkov and the Prince but did not enter into conversation with them.

I saw Liza three times in all: once in a milliner's shop with her mother, once in an open carriage with her father, mother, and the Prince, and once in church. Needless to say, I did not dare to approach her and only looked upon her from afar. In the shop she was very anxious yet cheerful. . . . She was ordering something for herself and was busily trying on ribbons. Her mother was gazing at her with arms crossed and resting on her stomach, her nose in the air, and that stupid, devoted smile on her face which is allowed only for loving mothers.

On the second occasion Liza was in the carriage with the Prince. . . . I shall never forget that encounter! The old Ozhogins were sitting in the back seat of the carriage, with Liza and the

Prince up front. She was more pale than usual; two pink streaks were barely visible on her cheeks. She was turned halfway around, facing the Prince; supporting herself on her outstretched right hand (she was holding her parasol in her left hand) and listlessly bending her head, she was looking directly into his face with those expressive eyes of hers. At that moment she was surrendering her whole being to him, trusting him utterly and irrevocably. I did not have a chance to get a good look at his face—the carriage rushed past me too quickly—but it seemed to me that he too was deeply moved.

The third time I saw her was in church. It was no more than ten days since the day I had encountered her in the carriage with the Prince, no more than three weeks since the day of my duel. The Prince had long since finished the business which had brought him to the town of O——, but he continued to delay his departure: he informed Petersburg that he was ill. Every day the townspeople expected him to make a formal proposal to Kirilla Matveich. I myself was waiting only for this final blow so I could go away for good. The town of O—— had become loathsome to me.

I could not sit at home, and from morning till night I plodded about the neighborhood. One gray and cloudy day, as I was returning from a walk that had been cut short by the rain, I stopped into the church. The evening service had just begun; not many people were there. I looked around and suddenly saw a familiar profile sitting near a window. At first I did not recognize it: that pale face, that blank look, those sunken cheeks—could this really be the Liza I had seen two weeks ago? Wrapped up in a cloak, wearing no hat on her head, illuminated on one side by a cold beam of light coming through a broad, white windowpane, she was staring motionlessly at the iconostasis; she seemed to be engaged in a struggle to pray, a struggle to escape from some dark fear. A fat servant boy with red cheeks and yellow patterns across his chest was standing behind her, his hands folded behind his back; he was looking at his mistress with sleepy bewilderment. I was shaking all over and started to go up to her, but I stopped short. A torturous foreboding gripped my chest. Liza did not move until the very end of vespers. The whole congregation left, a cantor started to sweep out the church, and still she did not budge from her spot. The servant boy went up to her, said something to her, and touched her dress; she looked around, passed her hand over her face, and left. I escorted her, from a distance, to her house and then went home.

"She is ruined!" I exclaimed as I entered my room.

To be honest, I do not know to this day what sort of sensations I felt then. I remember folding my arms, throwing myself onto the divan, and staring at the floor; but for some reason, I know not what, I seemed to feel some kind of satisfaction in the midst of my grief. . . . There is no way I would have admitted that, if I were not writing this just for myself. . . . I really had been torn apart by an agonizing, terrible presentiment . . . and, who knows, perhaps I would have been taken aback if it had not been fulfilled.

"Such is the human heart!" some middle-aged Russian teacher would exclaim at this point in a voice full of importance, raising high a plump forefinger adorned with a ring made of carnelian; but what do we care about the opinion of a Russian teacher with a voice full of importance and a carnelian ring on his finger?

Be that as it may, my forebodings turned out to be justified. The news suddenly spread through town that the Prince had left, apparently because of an order received from Petersburg; that he had left without making any kind of proposal to Kirilla Matveich or to his wife; and that Liza would go on mourning his treachery until the end of her days. The Prince's departure had been entirely unexpected—as early as the evening before he left, his coachman, according to my servant, had not in the least suspected his master's intentions. The news threw me into a fever; I immediately got dressed and was about to run to the Ozhogins, but after thinking it over, I decided it would be more appropriate to wait until the following day.

I did not lose anything, however, by staying home. That very evening a man named Pandopipopulo hurriedly came to see me. He was a Greek traveler who had accidentally been stranded in O——; a gossip of the first order, he, more than any of the others, had felt nothing but a burning indignation against me for my duel with the Prince. He did not even give my servant time to announce him and all but forced his way into my room, gave me a vigorous handshake, begged a thousand pardons of me, called me a model of generosity and fortitude, painted the Prince in the darkest of colors, and took no mercy on the elder Ozhogins, whom Fate, in his opinion, had justly punished; he even hit at Liza in passing, gave me a quick kiss on the shoulder, and ran off. Among other things, I found out from him that the Prince, *en vrai grand seigneur,* * had offered a rather cold reply to a delicate hint from Kirilla Matveich on the evening before his departure, saying that he had no intentions of deceiving anyone and that he was not thinking of getting married; then he got up and bowed, and that was the last they saw of him. . . .

The next day I set out for the Ozhogin home. When I showed up, the blear-eyed footman jumped from the bench in the anteroom like a flash of lightning; I ordered him to announce me. He ran off and then immediately returned; he told me to please enter,

*In truly lordly style.

that he had been ordered to invite me in. I went into Kirilla
Matveich's study. . . . Until tomorrow.

March 30. A frost.

And so I went into Kirilla Matveich's study. I would give anything
to anyone who could show me now the look on my face when that
esteemed official quickly threw on his Bukharan dressing gown and
came to greet me with open arms. I must have radiated an atmo-
sphere of modest triumph, condescending sympathy, and unlim-
ited generosity. . . . I felt as if I were another Scipio Africanus.*
Ozhogin was visibly embarrassed and depressed; he avoided making eye contact with me and fidgeted around where he stood. I also
noticed that he was talking in an unnaturally loud voice and was
generally expressing himself in very vague terms; vaguely but fer-
vently he begged my pardon, vaguely alluded to the guest's departure, added a few general and vague remarks about the deception
and inconstancy of earthly blessings, and then suddenly, feeling
the tears coming to his eyes, he hurriedly took a pinch of snuff,
probably to make me think there might be some other reason for
his weeping. . . . He used green Russian snuff, and as everyone
knows, that plant will make tears well up even in the most staid
old men, so that the human eye looks through them dimly and
senselessly for several minutes.

I, of course, was very careful about the way I treated the old
fellow; I inquired about the health of his wife and daughter and
then immediately and quite tactfully turned the conversation to
the fascinating subject of crop rotation. I was dressed as I usually

*Scipio Africanus (237–183 B.C.) was a Roman general and conqueror.

dress; but after I had been filled with a feeling of tender decency and gentle condescension, a fresh and festive sensation came over me, and I felt as though I were wearing a white waistcoat with a white tie to match. Only one thing troubled me: the thought of seeing Liza again. . . . Ozhogin himself finally suggested that we go to greet his wife. That kind but stupid woman was in a state of terrible confusion when she first saw me; but her brain was not capable of sustaining one and the same impression for very long, and so she quickly calmed down. At last I saw Liza. . . . She walked into the room. . . .

I had expected to find her a shamed and penitent sinner and had already given my face a most affable and reassuring expression. . . . Why should I lie? I truly loved her and thirsted for the happiness of forgiving her, of offering her my hand; but to my inexpressible surprise, she responded to my deep bow with a cold laugh, casually commented, "Oh, it's you," and immediately turned away from me. True, it seemed to me that her laughter was forced, and in any case, it did not go very well with her terribly emaciated face. . . . But I certainly had not expected such a reception. . . . I stared at her in astonishment . . . what a change had taken place in her! There was absolutely no resemblance between the child she had been and the woman she had become. She seemed to have grown taller, to have drawn herself up straighter; all her facial features, especially her lips, had assumed more definitive outlines . . . her gaze had become deeper, harder, darker.

I stayed with the Ozhogins until dinner; she got up a few times, left the room, and then returned; she calmly replied to questions and deliberately paid no attention to me. I could see that she wanted to make me feel as if I were not even worth her anger, even though I had very nearly killed her lover. I finally lost all patience: a venomous remark broke from my lips. . . . She shuddered, gave me a sharp glance, got up, went to the window, and in a slightly trembling voice muttered, "You can say what you like, but you must know that I love that man and shall always love him, and I don't blame him in the least for what he has done to me; on the contrary . . ." Her voice began to break, and she stopped to try to control herself but could not; she burst into tears and hurriedly left the room. . . . The elder Ozhogins were distressed by all this. . . . I shook hands with both of them, sighed, glanced up with a sorrowful look, and went away.

I am too weak and do not have enough time left; I am in no condition to describe in the former detail the new series of tormenting ruminations, the firm intentions, and other fruits of the so-called inner conflict which arose in me after I had renewed my relationship with the Ozhogins. I did not doubt that Liza still loved and would long continue to love the Prince, . . . and like a man tamed by circumstance and, indeed, tamed by himself, I did not even dream of her love; I longed only for her friendship, longed to win her trust, her respect, which, according to the testimony of experienced people, is considered the strongest foundation for happiness in marriage. . . . Unfortunately, I had lost sight of one rather small but important detail, namely that Liza had hated me since the day of the duel. I discovered this too late.

I began visiting the Ozhogin home as I had before. Kirilla Matveich showed me more kindness and affection than ever. I even have reason to believe that he would have gladly given me his daughter's hand, although I was not an envied suitor; public scandal followed him and Liza around, while I, on the other hand, was praised no end. There was no change in the way Liza treated me: most of the time she did not say a word. She obeyed when she was asked to eat and showed no outward signs of her grief;

nevertheless, she was wasting away like a candle. Kirilla Matveich should be given credit for one thing: he showed her every possible consideration, while Mme Ozhogin simply ruffled herself up like an old hen whenever she looked at her poor child. Biz'menkov was the only person Liza did not avoid, but she did not say much even to him. Her parents treated him harshly, even rudely; they could not bring themselves to forgive him for acting as a second. But he continued to visit them as if he had never noticed their disfavor. He was very cold toward me, and for some strange reason I felt as though I were afraid of him.

This went on for about two weeks. Finally, after a sleepless night, I decided to clear up everything with Liza, to open up my heart to her and tell her that in spite of the past, in spite of all the rumors and gossip, I would consider myself the happiest man in the world if she were to honor me with her hand and restore to me her trust. All joking aside, I actually imagined that I was presenting an unparalleled example of generosity, as the literature anthologies put it, and that she would give her consent out of sheer amazement. In any case, I wanted to get everything out into the open with her and escape once and for all my state of uncertainty.

Behind the Ozhogin house there was a relatively large garden which ended in a small linden grove, neglected and overgrown. A very old Chinese-style arbor rose up in the middle of this grove; a large wooden fence separated the garden from a dead-end alley. Liza would stroll through this garden for hours on end all by herself. Kirilla Matveich knew this and kept an eye on her, giving orders that she was not to be disturbed. "Let her grief wear itself out," he said. When she could not be found in the house, all one had to do was ring the little bell on the porch just before dinner, and she would show up with some sort of crumpled leaf in her hand and the same stubborn silence on her lips and in her looks.

So one day, having noticed that she was not in the house, I pretended that I was getting ready to leave; I said good-bye to Kirilla Matveich, put on my hat, and went out from the anteroom into the courtyard, then from the courtyard into the street. But I immediately slipped back through the gate with extraordinary speed and made my way past the kitchen and into the garden. Fortunately, no one noticed me. Without pausing long to think, I went into the grove with hasty steps. Liza was standing on the path right in front of me. My heart pounded against my chest. I stopped for a moment, took a deep breath, and was just about to walk up to her, when all of a sudden, without turning around, she raised her hand to her ear and started to listen. . . . From behind the trees, in the direction of the blind alley, two hard knocks sounded out clearly, as if someone was rapping on the fence. Liza clapped her hands, the faint squeak of the wicket gate could be heard, and Biz'menkov emerged from the thicket. I quickly hid behind a tree. Liza silently turned toward him. . . . He silently took her by the arm, and the two of them quietly walked along the footpath. I looked at them in a state of shock. They stopped for a moment, looked around, disappeared behind the bushes, came out again, and finally went into the arbor.

This arbor was a tiny, circular structure with a door and one small window; in the center, propped up on one leg, was an old table, overgrown with fine green moss; along the sides were two faded wooden benches standing just a short distance out from the damp, shaded walls. They used to drink tea here in the old days on unusually hot afternoons, even if only once a year. The door would not close all the way; the shutter had long since fallen out of the window, and caught by one corner, it dangled there pitifully, like the wounded wing of a bird. I sneaked up to the arbor and cautiously peeked through a crack in the window. Liza was sitting on one of the benches with her head hanging down. Her right hand was lying in her lap, while Biz'menkov held her left hand in both of his. He was gazing at her with sympathetic eyes.

"How are you feeling today?" he asked her in a low voice.

"The same," she replied. "Neither better nor worse." Then, raising her eyes in a look of despair, she added, "Emptiness, terrible emptiness!"

Biz'menkov made no reply.

"Tell me," she went on, "do you think he'll write me again?"

"I don't think so, Lizaveta Kirillovna!"

She remained silent for a while.

"He really doesn't have anything to write about, does he? He told me everything in his first letter. I could not be his wife; but I was happy . . . for a short while . . . I was happy."

Biz'menkov lowered his eyes.

"Oh," she continued, now more animated, "if you only knew how repulsive that Chulkaturin is to me. . . . Every time I look at that man's hands I seem to see . . . his blood." (I stood mutilated behind the crack in the window.) "And yet," she added thoughtfully, "who knows, if it had not been for that duel, perhaps. . . . Oh, when I saw him wounded I felt right away that I was all his."

"Chulkaturin loves you," Biz'menkov remarked.

"What is that to me? Do I really need anyone's love?" She paused for a moment and then slowly added, "Except yours. Yes, my friend, I need your love: I would die without you. You have helped me to endure those terrible moments when. . . ."

She fell silent. . . . Biz'menkov began to stroke her hand with fatherly tenderness.

"There's nothing we can do about it, Lizaveta Kirillovna, nothing we can do!" he repeated several times over and over.

"Yes, even now," she muttered in a toneless voice, "I think

I would die without you. You are the only one who sustains me; more than that, you remind me of him. . . . You have known everything all along. Do you remember how handsome he looked that day? . . . But forgive me: it must be difficult for you. . . ."

"Speak, speak! What do you mean? God bless you!" Biz'menkov interrupted her.

She squeezed his hand.

"You are very kind, Biz'menkov," she went on. "You are as kind as an angel. What am I to do? I feel that I shall love him till I die. I have forgiven him, I am grateful to him. May God grant him happiness! May God give him a wife after his own heart!" Her eyes filled with tears, and after a brief pause she added, "If only he wouldn't forget me; if only he would remember his Liza from time to time. . . . Let's go out now."

Biz'menkov raised her hand to his lips.

"I know"—she began to talk excitedly—"that everyone is blaming me now, that they're all casting stones at me. Let them! I wouldn't exchange my unhappiness for their happiness anyway. . . . No! No! . . . He may not have loved me for long, but he loved me! He never deceived me; he never told me I would be his wife. I never even thought of it myself. My poor papa was the only one who hoped for that. Even now I am not completely unhappy; I still have the memory of it all, and no matter how terrible the consequences may be. . . . I'm suffocating in here. . . . This is where I saw him for the last time. . . . Let's go out into the air."

They got up. I scarcely managed to jump aside and hide behind the thick trunk of a linden tree. They came out of the arbor and, as far as I could tell from the sound of their footsteps, went off into the grove. I do not know how long I had been standing there nailed to the spot, immersed in some kind of absurd bewilderment, when I suddenly heard their footsteps once again. I gave a start and carefully peeked out from behind my hiding place. Biz'menkov and Liza were on their way back, walking along the same path. Both of them were very agitated, especially Biz'menkov. He seemed to have been crying.

Liza stopped, looked up at him, and distinctly pronounced the following words: "I give you my consent, Biz'menkov. I wouldn't do so if you simply wanted to save me, to rescue me from this terrible situation. But you love me; you know everything—and you love me: I shall never find a more trustworthy, faithful friend. I shall be your wife."

Biz'menkov kissed her hand; she smiled at him sadly and went to the house. Biz'menkov ran off into the thicket, and I went home. Since Biz'menkov had probably said to Liza exactly what I was going to say to her, and since she had given him the very answer that I had longed to hear from her, it was pointless for me to worry about it further. Two weeks later she married him. The old Ozhogins were glad to get any bridegroom.

So tell me now, am I not a superfluous man? Haven't I played the role of a superfluous man throughout this entire affair? As far as the role of the Prince is concerned . . . there is nothing more to be said; Biz'menkov's role is also easy enough to understand. . . . But I? How did I fit into all this? . . . I was nothing but a stupid fifth wheel on the cart! . . . Oh, how bitter, how very bitter it is to me! . . . And so, as the fellows who haul the barges say, "Heave ho, one more time!" One short day, and then another, and nothing will be bitter or sweet to me any more.

March 31

It's bad. I am writing these lines in bed. The weather has suddenly changed since last night. It is hot today, almost like a summer day. Everything is thawing, dripping, flowing. The air is filled with the smell of plowed earth; it is a heavy, powerful, stifling odor. Steam is rising from everywhere. The sun is beating down, pounding down. I am in a bad way. I feel like I am decomposing.

I wanted to write my diary, and what have I done instead? I have related a single incident in my life. I have been babbling; dormant memories have been awakened within me and have carried me away. I have written it down without haste, in detail, as though I still had years ahead of me; and now there is no time left. Death, death is on its way. I can already hear its terrible crescendo. . . . It is time. . . . It is time! . . .

And indeed, what does it matter? Does the story I have told make any difference? The last of the earthly vanities disappear in the face of death. I feel a calm coming over me; everything is becoming so simple, so clear to me. Too late I have come to my senses! . . . How strange it is! I am growing calm—it is true, and yet . . . I am terrified. Yes, I am terrified. Half leaning over the silent, yawning abyss, I shudder, turn away, and look all around with hungry attention. Every object is doubly dear to me. I cannot gaze enough at my poor, cheerless room, as I bid farewell to every tiny spot on my walls! Satiate yourselves for the last time, oh eyes of mine! Life is fading away; it is fleeing from me steadily and quietly, like the shore receding from the gaze of a seafaring trav-

DIARY OF A SUPERFLUOUS MAN

eler. The aged, yellow face of my nurse, bound up in a dark kerchief, the bubbling samovar on the table, the geranium in the flowerpot by the window, my poor dog Trezor, the pen with which I write these lines, this hand of mine, I see you now . . . there you are, there. . . . Is it possible that . . . perhaps today . . . I shall never see you again? It is painful for a living being to part with life! Why are you fawning over me, my poor dog? Why do you lean your breast against my bed, your short tail between your legs, never taking your kind, sad eyes from me? Can it be that you are sorry for me? Do you somehow sense that your master will soon be no more? Oh, if only I could go through all my memories in my mind, just as I run my eyes over all the objects in my room! I know these memories are unhappy and insignificant, but they are all I have. Emptiness, terrible emptiness! as Liza said.

Oh, my God, my God! I lie here dying. . . . My heart, ready and able to love, will soon cease to beat. . . . And is it possible that it will be silenced forever without having once experienced happiness, without having known the sweet burden of joy? Alas! It is impossible for me, impossible, I know. . . . If at least now, before my death—death, after all, is truly a sacred thing, for it elevates every being—if only some nice, sad, friendly voice would sing over me a farewell song, a song of all my sorrows, I would perhaps be reconciled to it all. But dying is lonely, stupid. . . .

I believe I am beginning to rave.

Farewell, life, farewell, my garden, and you, my lindens! When summer comes, see that you do not forget to cover yourself with flowers from top to bottom . . . and may people find it good to lie in your fragrant shade on the cool grass, beneath the rustling murmur of your leaves as they stir ever so slightly in the wind. Farewell, farewell! Farewell to everything and forever!

Farewell, Liza! I have written these two words—and have almost laughed. This exclamation strikes me as bookish. I seem to be writing a sentimental tale or the closing to a despairing letter. . . .

Tomorrow is the first of April. Can it be that I shall die tomorrow? In a way, that would be rather improper. It suits me nonetheless. . . .

Oh, you should have heard the doctor chatter today! . . .

April 1

It is finished. . . . My life is over. I shall surely die today. It is hot outside . . . almost stifling . . . or is it that my lungs are already refusing to breathe? My little comedy has been played out to the end. The curtain is falling.

In becoming annihilated, I shall no longer be superfluous. . . .

Oh, how bright the sun is! Those mighty beams of light breathe eternity. . . .

Farewell, Terent'evna! . . . As she sat by the window this morning, she started crying . . . perhaps over me . . . and perhaps because she herself will die soon. I made her promise "not to hurt" Trezor.

It is very hard for me to write . . . I keep dropping my pen. . . . It is time! Already I can hear death getting closer with a growing roar, like a carriage rumbling over the pavement in the night; it is here. It hovers around me, like that faint breath that made the prophet's hair stand on end. . . .

I die. . . . Live on, ye who live!

And at the threshold of the grave
May the young live and play,
And may indifferent nature
Eternally beam with beauty!

A note from the editor of Chulkaturin's diary. Under this last line there is the profile of a head with a large tuft of hair and a mustache, the eye looking straight ahead, and radiating eyelashes; and beneath the head someone has written the following words:

This manuscript has been Read
And the Contents Thereof Been Approved
By Petr Zudoteshin
M M M M
Dear Sir
Petr Zudoteshin
My Dear Sir.

But since the handwriting in these lines in no way resembles the handwriting in which the rest of the notebook is written, the editor believes himself justified in concluding that the aforementioned lines were added later by someone else; this conclusion is all the more justified by the fact that it has come to his (the editor's) knowledge that Mr. Chulkaturin actually died on the night of April 1–2, 18— at his native estate of Ovech'i Vody.

SELECTED BIBLIOGRAPHY

Dukas, Vytas, and Richard H. Lawson. *"Werther* and *Diary of a Superfluous Man." Comparative Literature* 21 (1960): 146–54.

Freeborn, Richard. *Turgenev: The Novelist's Novelist.* London: Oxford University Press, 1960.

Kagen-Kaus, Eva. *Hamlet and Don Quixote: Turgenev's Ambivalent Vision.* The Hague: Mouton, 1975.

Kurlyandskaya, G. B. *Khudozhestvennyi metod Turgeneva-romanista.* Tula, 1972.

Magarshack, David. *Turgenev: A Life.* New York: Grove Press, 1954.

Markovich, V. M. *Chelovek v romanakh I. S. Turgeneva.* Leningrad, 1974.

Ripp, Victor. *Turgenev's Russia.* Ithaca, NY: Cornell University Press, 1980.

Schapiro, Leonard. *Turgenev: His Life and Times.* New York: Random House, 1978.

Shatalov, S. E. *Khudozhestvennyi mir I. S. Turgeneva.* Moscow, 1979.

Yarmolinsky, Avrahm. *Turgenev: The Man, His Art and His Age.* New York: Octagon Press, 1977.